As an apple tree among the trees of the woods,

so is my lover among men.

I delight to rest in his shadow,

and his fruit is sweet to my mouth.

—Song of Solomon

an apple harvest

Recipes and Orchard Lore

Frank Browning and Sharon Silva

TEN SPEED PRESS
Berkeley

Published in the United States by Ten Speed Press,
an imprint of the Crown Publishing Group,
a division of Random House, Inc., New York.
www.crownpublishing.com
www.tenspeed.com

Ten Speed Press and the Ten Speed Press
colophon are registered trademarks of
Random House, Inc.

Originally published in hardcover in the United States
in a slightly different form by Ten Speed Press, an
imprint of the Crown Publishing Group, a division of
Random House, Inc, in 1999.

Library of Congress Cataloging-in-Publication Data
Browning, Frank, 1946-
  An apple harvest : recipes and orchard lore / Frank
Browning and Sharon Silva.
    p. cm.
  Includes index.
  ISBN 978-1-58008-446-8
  1. Cookery (Apples) 2. Apples. I. Silva, Sharon.
II. Title.
  TX813.A6B76 2010
  641.6'411—dc22

                            2010007911

First Paperback Edition

Printed in Singapore

Cover and text design by Nancy Austin
Food photography by Leigh Beisch
Food styling for interior and back cover photography
by Wesley Martin
Food styling for front cover photography
by Dan Becker
Prop styling by Carol Hacker

All apple identification photography (except as noted
below) by Scott Vlaun

Additional photography credits:
Photo of Pink Lady apple (page 35): courtesy of
Brandt's Fruit Trees, Washington; photo of Jonathan
apple (pages 32 & 91): courtesy of Stark Brothers.

10 9 8 7 6 5 4 3 2 1

CONTENTS

ACKNOWLEDGMENTS

We wish to thank a number of friends and acquaintances for their pomological insights and assistance: Nancy Austin, Cecilia Brunazzi, George Csicsery, Palma Csicsery, Judith Dunham, Elisabeth Dyssegaard, Ed Fackler, Susan Gimprich, Maggie Gin, Pascal Giraudeau, Erkan Gözüm, Annette Herskovits, Fred Hertz, Mary Hester, Gene Kahn, Max Koch, Mitch Lynd, Jennifer Lyons, Kirsty Melville, Peggy Merrifield, Lynn Meyer, Daniel Orr, Rebecca Pepper, Marc Sharifi, Bob Shaw, Gail Silva, Judy Stone, Toni Tajima, Frank Viviano, Bill Wagner, Molly Walker, Tuny Walker, Aaron Wehner, Dawn Yanagihara, and Matilda Young.

INTRODUCTION

Apples are, quite simply, the preeminent fruit of temptation. Their fragrant flowers lure us into the indolence of spring. The easy latticework of their sturdy limbs beckons us to climb high through twisted, curling branches. Their brash display of gold and crimson skins calls to us to stray and pluck them from the farmer's field, entering into a silent feast of autumn theft.

Greeks, Romans, Persians, Vikings, and Celts: for all of them the apple was the consummate symbol of concupiscence, of love, and even of immortality. Yet the apple remains the most ordinary and practical of fruits. Durable, it can fit into and survive the jostling of any child's knapsack. Hardy, it survives and flourishes in all but the most steamy or frigid climates. Flexible, its trees will bend and fit into almost any minimally fertile garden or field. Beguiling, it offers itself fresh as the symbol of childhood health and, distilled into Calvados, as a standard for the finest of brandies.

Apple orchards were, for most of the last millennium, everywhere. The Browning orchard, laid out along a ridgetop in eastern Kentucky, was one of four in our small county alone. Nearly every county with decent farmland had as many. Most of the old farmers kept at least a small personal orchard of a dozen trees just beyond the garden's edge. (The Silva farm, just north of San Francisco Bay, held some forty hunchbacked old trees, but more of that in a moment.)

Apples came to me, Browning, both as work and as poetry. The earliest work for my brother and me was tidying up the dirt-floored sales shed on Sunday mornings before the after-church onslaught. Sundays have always been big sales days for apple growers, even though all the regular stores are closed. Stuffed with sermons, mashed potatoes, and chicken and still dressed up, the families wound their way up the one-lane road to Pea Ridge, through the oak and poplar woods and into the clearing that was our orchard. Sometimes dusty traffic jams blocked the driveway, as pickup trucks and Pontiacs tried to squeeze between the banks where the old climbing roses grew.

Most of the money we had to live on for the year spilt out of the frayed wallets of those Sunday afternoon apple buyers. Our job, my brother's and mine, was to help the customers carry bushel bags of fruit out to the car and carefully stow them, four or five at a time, in the trunk.

The names of the apples—and we grew more than twenty different varieties—were as evocative as the dishes my mother concocted from them. Maiden Blush. Stayman Winesap. Winter Banana. King David. Rome Beauty. Black Twig. Transparent.

Could an apple be transparent? No matter. We waited like pigs at the trough for the tart, green applesauce—the first of the year, around Independence Day—that came from the stewing and sieving and chilling of those early Transparents. The Maiden Blush apples were as delicate as the name suggested, a fair blond fruit kissed by a patch of pink, which since Jefferson's days at Monticello were favored as a drying apple. And those dark, ruby-skinned King Davids, their yellow flesh shot through with veins of crimson, quartered and roasted alongside a rolled pork roast, stood like a calendar marker of autumn's arrival: they were small, modest apples, but hidden within was a flavor as rich and regal as any king might imagine. Winter Bananas? A giggle of a name. We had only a few trees and just as few customers who cared for the big, knobby, yellow November fruit.

Everybody, however, wanted Winesaps: the dark "old-fashioned" or "Virginia" Winesaps that never failed to make a crop (and were so small they never failed to drive the pickers mad) and the large, dusky pink Staymans that were the most popular of anything we grew. There, in dry, teetotaling eastern Kentucky, where real wine was seen as little better than the Devil's vintage, the very sound of the word—*Winesap*—spun for me a wondrous image of epicurean indulgence that flourished somewhere beyond our spare life on the ridge.

Black Twigs, their thick, slightly bitter, scruffy skin enveloping a sweet-sour flesh, seemed like sterner fruit, good for a winter pocket but somehow linked to the threat of a hickory switch for errands left undone.

*Browning, age 5,
in the orchard.*

Rome Beauty? Well, they were the hearts of those crusty apple dumplings served on winter nights with hard sauce, and that was good enough. For our Christian neighbors (who called them Roman Beauties), I suppose they carried New Testament shadows. But I knew exactly what their name promised: future travels across the sea to the worn-out paths of ancient emperors. And each bite through the broken, buttery crust to the flesh within would carry me a moment closer to the imagined day of my own arrival in that eternal city beneath the Mediterranean sun.

All such daydreams aside, there were mostly the pedestrian chores of helping out in the orchard. Lacing poison along the grassy trails of field mice, which otherwise would burrow into the winter soil and chew away the roots of the trees. Thinning the over-set marble-sized fruits in early June so the apples that remained would grow large and pretty. And later, as we grew older, we were enlisted to pick the apples. ("Didn't I tell you to be careful picking Goldens! Place them in the picking bag. Don't drop them! They bruise!") Longer, it seemed, than any other farmers' crops, apple work began in February: pruning, followed by the first sprays of dormant oil and sulfur, followed by the anxieties of April bloom when rain could drive away the pollinating bees or frost could kill the fragile blossoms, only to end the following January when we'd sold the last Romes and Black Twigs, which, somehow, we had managed to save from freezing.

These were the tastes, traditions, and childhood fantasies of Browning's eastern apples, the lore born of early American naturalists like Henry David Thoreau and Thomas Jefferson.

The first Silva in America knew nothing of Thoreau and Jefferson, and, in the beginning, knew nothing of apples either. In the early 1880s, my tough, bandy-legged grandfather left the poverty of the Azores, volcanic fragments of Portugal adrift in the Atlantic, for the promise of prosperity in California. He had been born on the fertile island of Faial amid pineapple, chestnut, and banana trees, but didn't remember any Reinettes or Russets, Calville Blancs or Cox's Orange Pippins. Nor was his new home, in southern Sonoma County, serious apple country, but his neighbors all had at least a few trees, and by the turn of the century, he did too.

Over the decades, our land shifted with the local economy, moving from sugar beets to truck farm to dairy cows to hay and grain. By the time I came along in the 1940s, those early apple trees were twisted with age. But they still produced a good crop, due mostly to friends with commercial orchards in the northwestern part of the county who came each year to prune and graft, ensuring a healthy flush of blossoms. Half a dozen trees stood around my grandparents' house: a couple alternating with the prettier black walnuts along the driveway; two others, along with an apricot, shading the six-foot-high aviary that was home to a chorus of singing canaries and finches; and the last two joining a nearly equally ancient quince and fig between the house and the chicken yard. One more, the survivor of a fire in the 1920s that destroyed the original rosebush-covered family home, stared across at the well-worn redwood barn.

HORTA, Fayal, Açores

Some of the Silva family on the farm, a few decades past.

But the biggest stand of apple trees was a hundred yards or so from the small wood-frame house where my sister and I were raised, just down the lane from my grandparents' place. About forty trees flourished there, protected on one side from rising winter floodwaters by a eucalyptus-lined levee and on the other by the gentle incline of the Sonoma foothills. My grandfather called them simply *macãs*—apples. Not Gravensteins. Not Jonathans. Not McIntoshes. And to this day their proper names are a mystery to me.

Just before the first sign of buds in the spring, when the branches were little more than scaffolds, a local beekeeper would install several pale gray wooden hives under the trees. I stayed out of the orchard then and looked forward to apple blossom honey. Once the fruit began to set, the hives were uprooted, swept free of their treasures, and set down in new quarters beneath the lanky eucalyptus.

My sister and I always raided the apple trees—in fact, all the fruit trees—early, before their fruits had ripened. The birds were formidable competitors, and we were determined to beat them. We would pluck the hard, homely fruits from the branches, immediately peel away their rugged skins with our pocketknives, and then happily eat them in place. We loved the crispness and sourness of a premature harvest, even though we sometimes paid for it with stomachaches and parental finger wagging. Once the apples had ripened, our mother would line up lugfuls of them along the cool side of the house and can quarts of applesauce and fry batches of sugar-dusted fritters for Sunday supper. Next door, our grandmother would spread the apples on the cold floor of her cellar and in the unused corner of the nearby creamery until she had the time to can, and then she would devote a whole day to topping off Mason jars with fragrant apple butter.

Late summer promised the arrival of the hay press crew, who took up temporary residence on cots on the first floor of the barn, and a funky mobile cook shack that harbored their traveling chef. A salty old fellow with curious tattoos, he baked the most handsome apple pies I have ever seen and left them to cool—and to tempt—on the drop-down shelf that stretched along one side of his compact kitchen. After lunch, when the workers returned to the fields, he would carve out a slice from a half-eaten pie and carefully balance it in my hands, a delicious wedge of sustenance to carry me through my afternoon chores.

My grandfather returned to the Azores only once, in the 1920s, sailing there with stories of the opportunity America offered. And although he still knew nothing of Jefferson or Thoreau, of Monticello or Walden Pond, he now did know something of *macãs*, a scrap of knowledge that gave him a small foothold in the lore of the American apple orchard.

Sharon Silva,
age 3 or so, asleep
on the farm.

A Brief History of the Fruit of Temptation

If apples are nearly everywhere in the New World and the Old, they are not all uniformly delicious. Of the six thousand or so identified varieties, only a few hundred are good enough to be swallowed. Most are little green knots, their scant sugars drowned in bitter acid. The native North American apples—four species of crabs stretching from Alaska to Cape Cod—are barely appealing to the birds. The apples we eat today are, like so much else, a gift of the Silk Route, that ancient trail of the caravans that transported so many delights of China, India, and Mongolia to the fledgling civilizations of the Mediterranean and eventually to the furry tribes of northern Europe. These apples, identified as *Malus domestica* by botanists, first arose on the slopes of the Tien Shan, or Heavenly Mountains, of modern Kazakhstan probably about ten thousand years ago.

The Persians seem to have been the first in recorded Western history to bring the apple both into the garden and onto the banquet table—apparently well before the ninth century B.C., if we are to judge from Homer's description in the *Odyssey*. Their walled gardens, called *pairidaeza*, from which we eventually derived the word *paradise*, contained pears, grapes, nut trees, flowering shrubs, and apples. The horticultural riches so impressed the Greek armies that they borrowed the concept and made it their own. The *pairidaeza* became the household center for alfresco dining and entertaining, as important for its design as for the food it produced.

Persian cuisine, reflecting the Persian spiritual pursuit of harmony through the balance of opposing forces, revered apples for their own balance of sweetness and tartness, and that culinary tradition continues to this day. Apples have long been chopped or sliced and mixed with beef or lamb (page 96) to produce rich, complex main dishes, or the same meats, ground and seasoned, are stuffed inside hollowed-out apples (page 92) and roasted with a vinegar basting sauce. That marriage of apples and meat, which eventually included pork, moved westward to the Roman kitchens and came to permeate the territories of the empire as recorded in Marcus Gavius Apicius's *Ars magirica*:

> *In a heavy pot, pour some oil and add garum [a briny flavoring produced by squeezing the liquid from salt-pickled mackerel], broth, chopped leek and coriander, and pieces of cinnamon bark. Chop small a leg of pork cooked with its skin. Simmer all together. Halfway through the cooking add Matian [a sweet Roman variety from which the Spanish word for apple,* manzana, *is derived] apples cored and cut into pieces. While the stew is cooking, pound pepper, cumin, green coriander or coriander seeds, mint, and wild carrot root. To this mixture*

add a combination of vinegar, honey, garum, a little cooked wine [brandy], and meat juices

from the pot, and work all together with a little vinegar. Bring it to the boil, then thicken with

crumbled pastry, season with pepper, and serve.

The finest apples were reserved for the so-called second table that followed the rich courses in Persian and Greco-Roman banquets. Perhaps more than all the other fruits, apples were valued for their "digestive" properties. Early epicureans believed that the clean, fresh balance of sugar and acid brought a healthy conclusion to the evening, a tradition that even today distinguishes southern French and Italian desserts from the pies and cakes favored by northern Europeans and Anglo-Saxons. No less a figure than Plutarch, describing the Greek palate, wrote, "No other fruit unites the fine qualities of all the fruits as does the apple. For one thing, its skin is so clean when you touch it that instead of staining the hands it perfumes them. Its taste is sweet and it is extremely delightful both to smell and to look at. Thus by charming all our senses at once, it deserves the praise that it receives."

As complex as the myths that swirled around them, apples also played a varied role among doctors and pharmacists, a role that shifted dramatically as the empire collapsed and the Dark Ages fell across Europe. Were it not for the Cistercian monasteries that preserved the horticultural art of grafting (through which all apple varieties are propagated), the sweet, delicious apples the Romans enjoyed would likely have disappeared as the Goths obliterated the great farming estates. What survived at large were seedling varieties, generally fermented as ciders. For the most part, they were bitter and inedible and therefore may have contributed to the widespread fear of eating fresh, uncooked apples that lasted late into the Renaissance. Sour apples, particularly those that ripen in summer, were generally believed to cause flux, or indigestion, and diarrhea. English monks were encouraged to consume ten raw apples a day during Lent to avoid constipation, while in the view of the Italian physician's handbook, *Regimen sanitatis*, sweet apples would stimulate the heart.

At the opening of the ninth century, Charlemagne decreed that every town should plant both early- and late-bearing apples of sweet and sour varieties, including such favorites as Gozmaringa, Geroldinga, Crevadella, and Spirareia.

The northern Europeans and the English had to wait until after the sixteenth century and the rise of horticultural science married to

nationalism for the apple to reclaim its culinary elegance. Both French and English agricultural scientists began breeding new varieties to meet the tastes of the fussy nobility. At Versailles, apples, like oranges, were being bred for their size, color, and shapeliness. French cuisine was flourishing, and along with it came the fine wines of Burgundy and Bordeaux. In England, however, attention focused on the creation and blending of specialty "hard" or fermented ciders, some of which the English claimed produced a finer fruit wine than anything bottled in France. "I hope that every English man; or Native of this Isle on his return hither will conclude with me, that our British Fruits yield us the best beverages, and of these Fruits the Apple the best, which is here called Cider," wrote the English horticulturist John Worlidge.

Apples became the preserve of the pastry chef in both England and France. While the ancients seldom cooked apples as a dessert—indeed, desserts in the modern sense were rare except in Persia—French technique produced shimmering tarts and subtly seasoned compotes, and the English gave us hearty double-crusted pies and crumbles. Apples might find their way into the gullet of a suckling pig or the cavity of a roasted fowl, but they gradually lost their place in the sort of savory cooking that persisted down the Rhine and the Danube to the Dardanelles and the Middle East. Across the ocean in America, apples turned up as midday snacks and in hearty winter sweets. In France, only the Norman and Breton cooks, for whom wine was a luxury, retained apples—and specifically hard cider—at the center of the meal. In Spanish Catalonia, spicy apple-meat sauces survived alongside sweet fruit desserts, and on the north coast, Asturian cuisine still uses the local hard ciders in everything from shellfish to sausage dishes. (It is from Asturias, where Celtic peoples were fermenting wild crab-like apples when the Romans first arrived, that modern French and English cider making is derived.)

Pharmacists in ancient Persia offered the following as an aphrodisiac for women: nine apple seeds ground together with whiskers from a man who had been brutally killed, a few grains of barley retrieved from a grave, the blood of a worm, of a black dog, and of the second finger of the left hand, mixed with semen and stirred into a glass of wine.

From mythic symbol of temptation to primitive diarrhetic, from effervescent elixir to wholesome dessert plate, apples have persisted and flourished throughout the world. A relative latecomer to the Pacific Basin, apples have become such a mainstay of fresh fruit markets that China is now the world's biggest producer and exporter, with more than five million acres planted, and its biggest consumer. The ever-evolving array of apple eaters around the world and their techniques for preparing the forbidden fruit are what has led us to prepare this guide to apple cookery old and new, near and far.

Choosing Your Apples:
Type, Purpose, Location, and a Word on Antiques

"I want some cookin' apples and I want some eatin' apples," the customers would tell us every fall when they came to the Browning orchard, and of course they expected us to tell them what to buy. Instead, we asked the customer, "What are you going to cook?" or "What do you like to eat—sweet apples or tart ones?" Arguably the very best applesauce apple is the old-fashioned Transparent or its more modern cousin, the Lodi. A good choice beyond that is the small, early autumn yellow apple called Grimes Golden, which is both tart and slightly nutty. McIntosh and all its kin—Cortland, Macoun, JerseyMac, Empire—are rather sweeter, but they break down after ten or twelve minutes of simmering in the saucepan. A Golden Delicious, on the other hand, holds its shape, as do York, Granny Smith, Jonagold, Braeburn, Rome Beauty, and, to some degree, Jonathan. A few, like Pink Lady and Arkansas Black, hold up even under pressure cooking. Generally, the more acidic apples tend to break apart more quickly than others, although in the case of the Newtown Pippin and the Granny Smith that isn't true, and semisweets from the Mac family break up easily. For a general guide to apple characteristics, check the illustrated Pomarium beginning on page 23.

Location, location, location. Where your apples are grown can make an enormous difference in how they taste. In its native Appalachia—particularly on the banks of the Ohio River in northern West Virginia, where it was found about a hundred years ago—the Golden Delicious is unsurpassed: crisp, slightly nutty, squirting with juice. And usually dusted with a bit of russet on its bright yellow skin and occasionally bearing a pink cheek. But a Golden grown in the Yakima Valley of Washington State or in southwestern France picked firm enough for cold storage has all the lure of a Styrofoam Christmas ornament. Likewise, snap a deep red McIntosh from the tree in Massachusetts, New York State, or Ontario, and it's like walking with Thoreau past Walden Pond in the 1840s, as the complex play of honeyed, tart, and spicy juices trickle down your throat. Pull one from a tree in Kentucky or California, however, and you'll find it immediately forgettable. Yet a Fuji properly harvested near Modesto or Stockton, sweetening slowly under the nearly endless

California sun, explodes with flavor. Food scientists in American universities persistently deny that soils make much difference in the flavor of the fruits grown on them, but common experience (and a few hundred years of French wine-making history) tells us that even one low-lying field may differ from another one on the same slope.

Then there are the antiques. It's true that a hundred years ago American fruit nurseries offered upward of eight hundred different apple varieties to farmers. Today perhaps fifty varieties are easily available from commercial nurseries, and only twenty-five or thirty are in good supply. Far too many of these are strains of the glamorous, but usually tasteless, Red Delicious. One response has been to elevate so-called antique apples to nearly reverential status. Many old apples are startlingly delicious: Cox's Orange Pippin in England; Calville Blanc and Reinette in France; Baldwin, King David, Esopus Spitzenburg, Mother, and Newtown Pippin in the United States. But far more fall into what antique apple specialist Tom Burford of Virginia calls "quick spitters," apples so dreadful you spit them out before swallowing. Most antique varieties have disappeared for good reason: they were difficult to grow, they were susceptible to disease (and there may be twenty times as many pests and diseases plaguing apples in today's travel-integrated world as there were a century ago), they bore poorly, or they didn't taste good. Tastes also change. In the 1950s, few apple eaters expected to have hard, crisp apples after Christmas. Stayman Winesap, Rome, and several of the Russets remained firm and lasted through the winter, but they were not crisp for more than three weeks after picking. Today apple-preference surveys show that Americans judge apples first by crispness, second by juiciness, and third by flavor. As a result, new varieties winning favor are Fuji, Braeburn, Suncrisp, Pink Lady, Pacific Rose, Jazz, and Temptation—any one of which will match or exceed the charms of the nineteenth century's revered antiques available from specialty nurseries.

Keeping Your Apples

Furniture makers say that a fine cherry board continues to live and breathe long after the tree has been cut and milled. The same is true of fruit. Apples continue to respire, to oxidize, in the presence of oxygen. As they do so, they release ethylene gas, which itself hastens ripening. The clearest evidence of this process is what happens when you leave apples in a refrigerator drawer with leafy greens: the greens quickly turn yellow.

Commercial orchards and packinghouses chill and store apples in nitrogen gas, a practice called controlled atmosphere (CA). In effect the apples are held in suspended animation for up to nine months; respiration stops. They are as crisp when they emerge as the moment they were stored, and they will remain so for about a week. As humans cannot breathe in a nitrogen atmosphere, we don't keep such rooms in our homes. A century ago in Michigan and New England, some apple farmers would seal the fruit in a barrel, then go out on a well-frozen pond, cut a hole in the ice, and submerge the barrel below the ice. It was said to be cheap and effective. Today the best most consumers can do is to approximate conventional cold storage, in which apples are held at 32°F under 100 percent humidity. We advise placing apples in a plastic bag, sprinkling them with water, punching a couple of holes in the bag, and keeping it in the coldest part of the refrigerator.

A traditional method for preserving snack and cooking apples is to slice them in thin rounds or wedges during the hot, arid days of late August or September and then dry them in the sun. If gnats and flies are a problem, spread a sheet of sheer cotton over the sliced fruit. Or you can place the slices in a home dehydrator or on racks in the oven set to 175°F for about a day. If you like them chewy, take them out earlier; if you prefer brittle apple crisps, leave them in until they snap like a thick potato chip. For cooking, simmer them slowly in water, wine, hard or fresh cider, bourbon, rum, Calvados, or your own favorite elixir.

To Peel or Not to Peel

Browning and Silva are of two minds on the all-important issue of when to peel the noble fruit. Silva usually prefers to peel. Browning adamantly advises against peeling unless a glaze or caramel coating is desired.

The Browning Approach: Because so much of the apple's flavor resides in its skin, including the tannins that give it that slightly bitter edge, I like to leave the skin on whenever possible. Double-crusted pies are not only prettier because of the rose color that leaches into the flesh from the skin, but their flavors are also more complex. Applesauce is all but worthless if made from peeled apples. The same is true for stuffings for poultry or meats, for fried apples, or for dishes like the Danish *aeble flaesk* (apples, potatoes, and bacon) or German *Himmel und Erde* (apples, potatoes, and blood sausage), both of which have traditionally been made with peeled apples. The further advantage of not peeling is that it helps hold the apple chunks together. There are, of course, occasions to peel. Open-faced tarts and galettes or a *tarte Tatin* are prettier if the whole apple slice can be glazed or caramelized. Yet one trick for a tastier Tatin is to peel the apple quarters that rest on the caramelized sugar and then to pile unpeeled apple pieces on top. Since the tart will be inversed at serving, the peeled apples won't show, and the flavor will be more intense.

One warning: The skins of some apples are simply too thick, bitter, or tough for anything except baking or applesauce. These include Arkansas Black, Black Twig, Virginia Winesap, and a handful of scarce old-timers not generally available. The easiest way to tell is to taste them while peeling.

The Silva Approach: More than once, while standing at my kitchen sink and peeling an apple, I have watched Browning grab a fallen curlicue, wrap it around a nude fruit wedge, and eat it, his blue eyes a pair of deep, steady disapproving pools. Although he feels that only a handful of apples are saddled with tough skins, I think they nearly all are. I am happy to leave those leathery hides in place for applesauce or sorbet because I know they will catch in the disk of the food mill. But I don't want them attached to my fritters, filling my pies, or punctuating my Waldorf salad. They stay on baked apples, of course, and on whole or quartered fruits lodged in the cavity of a roasting bird, but they come off for apple stuffings. Maybe my peeling arm was so well developed in my youth, when crop dusters regularly circled our land, that reaching for a knife is pure habit. What I do know is that while on a short residence in Europe, I was among a continent of peelers and felt right at home.

In the end, however, Browning has won more than his share of our arguments over whether a recipe should call for the peeled or the unpeeled. But since he grew up among rows of apple trees and I grew up among fields of grain, it seems only right to defer to his greater experience.

Cider Cookery

Ciders are as mysterious in their origins as the myths of temptation that surround their mother, the apple. In fact, the word itself may well predate the use of apples as the source of cider, for the early Jews called any strong drink that was not wine *shekar*, a term that traveled to the Greeks as *sikera*. At the same time that the diverse peoples of the eastern Mediterranean were fermenting an array of fruits, the Basques seem to have been making something from apples that they called *sizra*. And it is from the Basques and the Asturians that we inherited the modern fermented apple juice we call cider. Chances are the Celts were fermenting honey-sweetened apple juice as early as anyone else in the Western world, and as soon as they were able to make ciders, there's little doubt they were using cider for cooking.

The term *cider* requires a clarification. Everywhere in the world except the United States, cider or *cidre* or *sidra* means *fermented* apple juice. Like wine, sometimes the cider may be sweet, sometimes it may be dry, and sometimes it may be semisweet or semidry. It may be bubbling with effervescence, or it may be as still as an underground pool. But it is always a fermented beverage. Indeed, until the arrival of modern refrigeration, unfermented fruit drinks were relatively rare in the world.

American usage, however, has confused the meaning of this simple word. Over the last hundred years in the United States, cider has come to be interchangeable with raw, unfiltered apple juice. The reason is that nasty episode of the 1920s and 1930s: Prohibition. Although Washington, Jefferson, Adams, and later all of the friends and followers of John Chapman (aka Johnny Appleseed) kept dedicated cider orchards planted with apple varieties suitable for making fermented cider, a convergence of forces purged cider from the American palate during the nineteenth and twentieth centuries. First came the temperance movement of the 1840s, followed close on by German immigrants who brought beer to the growing cities of the Midwest. Grain was easier to store than apples, enabling beer to be made on site. The taste for cider dwindled everywhere in America and Europe save in the British Isles, spots of Germany, northwestern France, and northern Spain.

In America, cider presses were so deeply ingrained in popular rural memory, however, that any beverage flowing from them retained the name. After World War I, when refrigeration became readily available to the middle class, farmers began again to press their apples and sell the juice as sweet cider, a beverage not to be confused with the prohibited "hard," or alcoholic, cider. Just why fermented cider came to be called hard is contested. Some argue that it is the hard broken head that follows too much consumption of the bubbly brew, although most hard ciders seldom exceed the 5 or 6 percent alcohol content of beer. A counter-explanation suggests that the term derives from the small, hard apples generally found in varietal cider orchards. Most real cider apples, with names like Chisel Jersey, Brown Snout, Stokes Red, Dabinett, or Tremlett's Bitter in England and Bedan, Binet Rouge, Marin Oufrey, or Noël de Champs in France, are small and hard, and they are frequently bitter because of the high amounts of tannin in their skins. For drinking or cooking, ciders made from these apples are far superior to those made from common dessert and cooking apples.

"I remembered the nectareousness of the new cider, which I used to sip through a straw in my boyhood, and I never doubted that this would be as dulcet, but finer and more ethereal..."

—Nathaniel Hawthorne,
French and Italian Notebooks, 1858

Hard cider has begun to creep back into the American beverage pantry. Sadly, most of the commercially available ciders are light, frothy affairs pressed from culled or leftover table apples. A few made in New England and California have begun to use old, forgotten American cider varieties or English and French ones grafted from special collections like the National Apple Germplasm Repository at Geneva, New York.

As a cooking base, cider tends to follow the rules for white wines. Drier ciders work well for fish poaching and in marinades. Semidry or semisweet ciders will likely have a richer, more appley flavor and will work better in desserts and sweet sauces. Simple so-called fresh cider, best purchased directly from the grower or at a farmers' market, can be used with winter squashes, sparingly in meat stews, and in some sweet and savory sauces and desserts.

Cider Vinegar

Most of us probably remember cider vinegar from childhood Easter egg painting, with all the food coloring and little dishes and wire rings and the vinegar stinking up the kitchen. For serious cookery, quality vinegars usually are made from wine. We wouldn't pretend that a truly grand vinegar can be made from apple cider any more than we'd insist that the best *cidre bouché du Pays d'Auge* is the equal of a Pavillon Blanc du Château Margaux. But don't sell cider vinegar short. If the industrial stuff smells like a lab experiment gone wrong, homemade, or specialty, cider vinegars can be delightful and full of apple bouquet.

The first delicious cider vinegar I tasted was made by Mrs. Humphries, who lives down the road from the Browning orchard and has spent most of her life working on it. I liked her vinegar so much that, when I started fermenting cider, I'd hold some of the less promising stuff aside and expose it to fresh air through a cheesecloth cover. Sure enough, in a few weeks it would make a fine fruity vinegar. An important caution for the home cider maker is to keep your vinegar making far, far away from your unbottled fermenting cider; otherwise the plucky little *Micoderma aceti* bacteria will slip into your cider vat and turn the whole batch.

On the farm we made a number of specialty cider vinegars: with sage and dried ginger, with mixed herbs, with red raspberries. You can do the same: simply add the flavorings or berries to small bottles of vinegar and leave them to sit for a week or so.

One note about homemade vinegar: It gradually forms a thick, gray gummy mat—called a "mother"—across the top that's not too handsome when poured on your salads. If you like the flavor of your vinegar, remove the mother and store it with some of the vinegar in a tightly closed jar placed in a dark spot, like a cupboard or cellar. Then, for your next batch of vinegar, you can speed up the process by adding a bit of the stored mother to fresh or fermented cider. To prevent any more mother from growing on the original batch, heat the remaining vinegar to 160°F, which kills the *Micoderma aceti*, and add any flavorings you like.

Calvados and Applejack

Historically, farmers in the Calvados region of Normandy put aside a small amount of their cider each year for distillation as a sort of savings account, just as their fellow Cognac makers to the south did. The result was the grand, double-distilled apple brandy named for the region. The Calva' was allowed to age undisturbed in oak barrels, with newer vintages gradually added to older ones. If a crop failure occurred, the farmer would bottle up the fiery brandy and sell it off to pay the bills, with older batches fetching a finer price than the younger blends.

Good Calvados should be at least eight years old before bottling, fine Calvados at least fifteen. Truly grand Calvados may be thirty to forty years old and will likely sell for $250 to $600 a bottle. You wouldn't want to use it to flavor calf's liver.

Cooking with Calvados, or the cheaper American apple brandy commonly called applejack, is almost identical to cooking with Cognac. A tablespoon or two is usually enough. If you want to reduce the alcohol content—or make a fancy show—allow the Calva' to get hot in the pan. Then either light it with a match or, if you're cooking over a gas flame, very carefully tilt the pan into the flame until the liquid laps the rim and the flame ignites the alcohol. Bear in mind, however, that burning off the alcohol—whether it's bourbon, Cognac, or Calvados—will reduce the intensity of the spirit's innate taste.

a culinary pomarium

Pomona was the Roman wood nymph who tended the orchards on the
Palatine Hill beside the Tiber. Each year she carefully nurtured the bitter green
apples into a rich palette of red, yellow, gold, and russet fruits filled with the sweet
fragrances of autumn. Today, some six thousand known apple varieties exist in the
world. These are some of the ones we like best, with notes on their qualities, primary
growing areas, and uses. Unless otherwise noted, they are available commercially in
the United States, although often only in regional farmers' markets. Seasons are
keyed to the Midwest, mid-Atlantic, and Northern California zones; ripening may
occur a little later in New England or earlier in warmer climates. Apples described as
large are usually 3 inches or more in diameter, while small ones measure 2 1/2 inches.
All others are medium-sized, traditionally about 2 3/4 inches in diameter. In tribute
to Pomona, we call our annotated list a Pomarium.

ARKANSAS BLACK—*Large, hard, mildly sweet. Excellent keeper; improves in cold storage. Late autumn. Good for eating raw. California, southern United States.*

BRAEBURN—*Crisp, light fragrance, sweet-tart. Good keeper. Autumn. Good for eating raw, frying, and pies. Australia, New Zealand, United States.*

CORTLAND—*Large, sweet, slightly tart undertone. Poor keeper. Late summer through early autumn. Good for eating raw (doesn't oxidize when cut) and for applesauce (breaks down in cooking). Northeastern United States.*

CALVILLE BLANC—*Very tart, full fragrance, rich flavor. Good keeper. Winter. Favored for tarts. France (dates to 1599).*

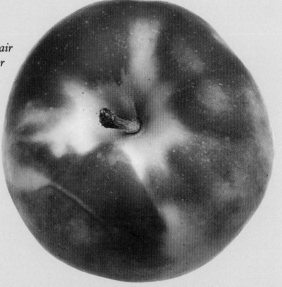

COX'S ORANGE PIPPIN—*Firm, somewhat crisp, complex sweet-tart-nutty. Fair keeper. Autumn. Good for eating raw and for all-purpose cooking. New Zealand, United Kingdom; poor in United States.*

ELSTAR—*Crisp, intense honeyed flavor. Good keeper. Late autumn. Good for eating raw and for desserts. Northern Europe.*

FUJI—*Crisp, juicy, very sweet, and fragrant (but only if the green undercolor has turned creamy yellow). Good keeper. Autumn. Good for eating raw, sliced and baked, and desserts. Worldwide.*

EMPIRE—*Crisp, mild, sweet-tart McIntosh cross. Moderate keeper. Early autumn. Good for eating raw and for all-purpose cooking (holds shape moderately well). Europe, United Kingdom, United States.*

GALA—*Sweet, moderately crisp and juicy, slightly spicy. Fair keeper. Late summer through early autumn. Good for eating raw and for desserts (holds shape well). Worldwide.*

GOLDEN DELICIOUS—*Rich, crisp, and juicy, honey-sweet if grown in eastern United States, bland and tasteless if grown in western United States and Europe. Fair keeper. Autumn. Good for eating raw, frying, and pies. Worldwide.*

GOLD RUSH—*Sweet-tart, similar to Golden Delicious but crispier. Good keeper; improves in cold storage. Late autumn. Good for eating raw, in stews, and for pies. Mostly Midwest.*

GRANNY SMITH—*Hard, crisp, tart, moderately juicy, modest flavor. Excellent keeper. Late autumn. Good for eating raw, frying, stews, and baking (very slow). Worldwide.*

HEWES CRAB—*Favored eighteenth- and nineteenth-century cider variety, high sugar, high acid, sharp, delicious flavor. Fair keeper. Late summer. Good for eating raw, roasting, and applesauce. Mostly Virginia.*

HONEYCRISP—*Large, crisp, bursting with juice, mellow-sweet, consistent winner in new taste tests. Good keeper. Late summer through early autumn. Good for eating raw, frying, roasting, and baking. North America, likely worldwide.*

JONATHAN—*Highly aromatic, sweet-tart. Fair to poor keeper. Early autumn. Good for eating raw, frying, roasting (holds shape moderately well), pies, and applesauce. Eastern United States.*

JONAGOLD—*Large, moderately crisp, very juicy, intensely sweet-tart cross of Jonathan and Golden Delicious. Moderate keeper. Early autumn. Good for eating raw, frying, roasting, and baking. Mostly Europe and northeastern United States.*

MCINTOSH—*Juicy, lightly crisp, blush of strawberry-raspberry aroma. Fair to poor keeper. Late summer through early autumn. Good for eating raw (doesn't oxidize when cut) and for applesauce (breaks down in cooking). Best in cold zones of northern United States and Canada and in northern Europe.*

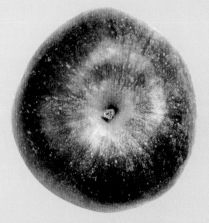

MACOUN—*Small, crispier, spicier cross of McIntosh. Fair to poor keeper. Autumn. Good for eating raw (doesn't oxidize when cut) and for all-purpose cooking. Treasured in upstate New York and lower New England.*

MUTSU—*Very large, crisp Golden Delicious offspring from Japan (also called Crispin in United States) with better flavor than western Golden Delicious. Moderate keeper. Early autumn. Good for eating raw, baking, and pies. United States, Asia.*

NEWTOWN PIPPIN—*Hard, crisp, tart, with bright, full flavor; favorite at Jefferson's Monticello. Excellent keeper; improves in cold storage. Late autumn. Good for eating raw, frying, roasting, and pies (holds shape well). Oregon.*

PINK LADY®—*Cripps Pink cultivar. Very crisp, sweet to slightly tart, hint of raspberry and kiwi; major new variety. Excellent keeper. Late autumn. Good for eating raw, frying, roasting, and pies (holds shape well). Australia, Mid-Atlantic, California, Asia.*

ROME BEAUTY—*Large, firm, mildly sweet; original Rome has superior taste to newer Red Rome. Good keeper but loses crispness. Autumn. Good for baking. Eastern United States.*

THE RUSSETS—*Roxbury, Golden, Ripston, Razer tend toward juicy, nutty, pearlike texture. Most are good keepers. Autumn. Good for frying, roasting, and applesauce. Rare except for France, New England, United Kingdom.*

STAYMAN WINESAP—*Initially crisp, juicy, tart-sweet, roselike fragrance. Good keeper but loses snap. Autumn. Good for eating raw and for all-purpose cooking. Virginia, Pennsylvania, New Jersey, Italy.*

SUNCRISP—*Crisp, juicy, honey-sweet. New and very promising cross of Cox's Orange Pippin with Golden Delicious. Excellent keeper. Late autumn. Excellent for eating raw, frying, and pies (holds shape well). Mostly Midwest but spreading nationwide.*

TRANSPARENT—*First summer apple, very tart. More common and very similar is Lodi. Poor keeper. Best choice for sharp, complex applesauce and "saucy" pies. Midwest, Mid-Atlantic, northeastern United States.*

the recipes

FIRST COURSES

Duck Breast and Fuji Apples on Watercress

I grew up not far from the legendary Reichardt Duck Farm, a quacking empire that sends hundreds of thousands of hormone-free birds to dinner tables every year. Founder Otto H. Reichardt, a man with an eye for a good-looking duck, acquired a small poultry farm in San Francisco at the turn of the last century, and soon after moved its stock of stately white Pekins to Sonoma County. In no time at all, Chinese restaurants up and down the state were clamoring for his fat, tender birds. I had never even seen a Muscovy until I saw the Seine, and even now I find it difficult to stray from a childhood memory, grabbing the Pekin over its Frenchified competitor for this simple salad. I suffer no sentiment when it comes to the apples, however, opting for a sweet newcomer, the Fuji, born in the late sixties, over the heirlooms. —SS

1 whole boneless Pekin or Muscovy duck breast with skin intact, 1 to 1¼ pounds

Coarse sea salt

Freshly ground pepper

1 teaspoon dried marjoram

4 to 5 cups young, tender watercress sprigs

2 tablespoons extra virgin olive oil

2½ tablespoons freshly squeezed Meyer or other lemon juice, or more to taste

2 Fuji or other sweet apples

Preheat the oven to 450°F.

Rinse the duck breast and pat dry. Cut in half along the line left by the breastbone, and trim away all visible fat. Season generously with salt and pepper and then rub evenly with the marjoram. Place in a small roasting pan, skin side up.

Roast for 18 to 20 minutes, or until the skin is golden brown and crispy and the meat is rare when cut into with a knife.

Meanwhile, place the watercress sprigs in a salad bowl. In a small bowl, whisk together the olive oil, 1½ tablespoons of the lemon juice, and salt and pepper to taste to form a dressing. Taste and adjust with more lemon juice if necessary.

Peel, halve, and core the apples, then thinly slice lengthwise. Place in a bowl and toss with the remaining 1 tablespoon lemon juice to coat evenly.

Drizzle the dressing over the watercress and toss to coat evenly. Divide among 4 plates, forming a bed on each. Arrange the apple slices on top, dividing them evenly and overlapping them in a neat row on each bed.

Remove the duck breast from the oven. Transfer to a cutting board and remove and discard the skin. Thinly slice the breast halves. Place one-fourth of the duck slices on each bed of apples, keeping each portion in its original shape as much as possible.

Season with salt and pepper and serve immediately.

SERVES 4

Winter Salad with Apples and White Cheddar

Soon after my brother married a New Englander, a prize delicacy started arriving in our Kentucky kitchen: sharp Cabot Cheddar cheese. That's when I learned about the Mason-Dixon rule of cheese. Yankees make it white; southerners want it orange. Without a moment's hesitation, I defected. Now good supermarkets everywhere stock Vermont cheeses. It's the combination of sweet and tart, tangy apples with puckery-sharp cheese that makes this salad. In summer, switch to butter or oak-leaf lettuce or the like, and use summer apples such as Tydeman Red, Gravenstein, Williams' Red, and Maiden Blush. Also note that McIntosh and Pink Lady tend not to oxidize (turn brown) as quickly as others and therefore look prettier longer. —FB

DRESSING

2¹/₂ tablespoons cider vinegar or white wine vinegar

6 tablespoons extra virgin olive oil or walnut oil

Salt

Freshly ground pepper

· · · · ·

1 small head radicchio, leaves separated and cut lengthwise into narrow strips

2 heads Belgian endive, leaves separated and cut lengthwise into narrow strips

1 small head frisée, tough stems removed and torn into small pieces

1 Newtown Pippin, Granny Smith, Stayman Winesap, or other tart apple, unpeeled, quartered, cored, and thinly sliced lengthwise

1 Fuji, Pink Lady, eastern Golden Delicious, McIntosh, or other sweet apple, unpeeled, quartered, cored, and thinly sliced lengthwise

¹/₂ cup walnut halves, toasted

Wedge of sharp white Cheddar cheese

To make the dressing, whisk together the vinegar and olive oil in a small bowl. Season with salt and pepper.

To make the salad, combine the radicchio, endive, and frisée in a large salad bowl. Toss well. Add the apples and nuts and drizzle with the dressing. Toss again. Using a vegetable peeler or sharp paring knife, shave curls of the Cheddar cheese over the top. Serve at once.

SERVES 6

Aunt Mae's Waldorf Salad

Aunt Mae, twice divorced, drifted back and forth between the farm and the city. She wanted to be an artist, but became a stenographer. She wanted to go dancing in nightclubs, but found herself in chicken coops wrestling eggs from beneath defiant hens. She wanted to eat in restaurants, but spent hours in front of my grandmother's stove. She turned our apple harvest into cinnamony applesauce, dark brown apple cakes, and this version of the Waldorf-Astoria classic. The original, created by Oscar Tschirky, a chef known for his distaste for gourmandizing, reportedly used only apples, celery, and mayonnaise. Aunt Mae dressed it up with what was at hand: walnuts, grapes, and pomegranate seeds from just beyond the front porch. —SS

MAYONNAISE

1 egg yolk

$1/2$ teaspoon Dijon mustard

$2^1/_2$ teaspoons freshly squeezed lemon juice, or more to taste

Salt

White pepper

6 tablespoons safflower oil

6 tablespoons mild olive oil

• • • • •

4 Fuji, Gala, or other sweet apples, peeled, halved, cored, and diced

Juice of 1 lemon

1 cup walnuts, toasted and coarsely chopped

$1/2$ cup finely chopped celery

$1^1/_2$ cups green or red seedless grapes, halved lengthwise

Pomegranate seeds for garnish (optional)

To make the mayonnaise, combine the egg yolk, mustard, 2 teaspoons of the lemon juice, and a pinch each of salt and white pepper in a bowl and whisk until blended. In a small pitcher, mix together the safflower and olive oils. Whisk the oils into the egg yolk mixture a drop at time. Once the mixture begins to thicken nicely, add the oils in a very slow, thin stream while continuing to whisk constantly. When the mixture is the consistency of mayonnaise, whisk in the remaining $1/2$ teaspoon lemon juice. Taste and adjust the salt, pepper, and lemon juice.

To make the salad, toss the apples with the lemon juice in a large bowl. Add the walnuts, celery, and grapes and toss to mix. Add about $2/_3$ cup of the mayonnaise and turn to coat evenly. Add as much of the remaining mayonnaise as needed to dress the mixture lightly. (Any leftover mayonnaise slides nicely onto bread for a lettuce and tomato sandwich.) Cover and chill before serving.

Just before serving, scatter some pomegranate seeds over the top.

SERVES 6 TO 8

Christmas Herring and Apples

On Christmas Eve in Denmark, traditionalists gather for a grand dinner and to sing holiday songs, walk around the tree, and then open their presents. The next morning everyone gets up late, takes a brisk walk, and then sits down to a multicourse lunch—trying to forget the big dinner they've eaten less than twenty-four hours earlier. Elisabeth Dyssegaard, a New York editor who grew up in a great, extended Danish family, remembers the annual herring salad that always launched the fish course. "The recipe was my great-aunt's, and my mother ate it every Christmas when she was a child. When her mother died, she began to make it. It is a dramatic purplish pink and is served with hard-boiled eggs, sliced in half, and thin, dark Danish rye. It's delicious."

Apples, which in the past were one of the few fruits available in winter, show up in all sorts of Danish recipes. Elisabeth offers a few provisos with respect to this dish: Use a crisp apple that holds its shape—we suggest Newtown Pippin, Pink Lady, Arkansas Black, or Braeburn—and choose a mild pickle or, for a special treat, home-pickled squash. And, she says, in her house the mustard had to be Colman's. In Denmark, the herring salad comes on its own plate, to be followed by sausages, smoked lamb, pâtés, and cheese—all of it washed down with sturdy beer and aquavit. —FB

DRESSING

2 tablespoons all-purpose flour

1 cup beet juice, or more as needed

2 to 3 teaspoons Colman's English dry mustard

1 teaspoon olive oil

Salt

· · · · ·

2 cups peeled and finely diced celeriac (celery root), parboiled for 2 to 3 minutes and drained (see note)

2 cups peeled, cored, and finely diced apple (see recipe introduction for suggested varieties)

2 cups finely diced mild dill pickle

2 cups well-drained, finely chopped herring fillet in clear brine (not in sour cream)

4 or 5 hard-boiled eggs, peeled and halved lengthwise

Thinly sliced dark rye bread for serving

To make the dressing, spoon the flour into a small bowl. Add a little of the beet juice and stir to form a paste. Gradually mix in up to 1 cup beet juice, stirring well to prevent lumps from forming. Pour into a small saucepan and bring to a simmer. Cook, stirring constantly, for 2 to 3 minutes to cook away the raw flour taste and to thicken to a nice consistency. Remove from the heat. If a few small lumps remain, pour the dressing through a sieve. Let cool.

While the mixture is cooling, mix the dry mustard with an equal amount of water to form a paste and let stand for 10 minutes. Then stir the mustard into the cooled

(continued)

(Christmas Herring and Apples, continued)

beet juice to taste. Add the olive oil (it gives the dressing a pretty sheen) and season with salt. If the dressing has thickened too much upon cooling, add a little beet juice to thin it.

To make the salad, combine the celeriac, apple, pickle, and herring in a large bowl and mix well. Add the dressing and turn all the ingredients to coat evenly.

Mound the dressed salad on a platter and surround with the egg halves. Serve with the dark rye.

SERVES 8 TO 10

NOTE: Celeriac discolors quickly upon peeling. If you are not immediately plunging the diced root into boiling water, toss it with a little freshly squeezed lemon juice to keep it from browning.

ARKANSAS BLACK

Traditional wassailing chant performed on Twelfth Night in Somerset, England, to encourage a bountiful new year:

Here's to thee, old apple tree.

May'st thou bud, may'st thou blow,

May'st thou bear apples enow!

Hat's full, caps full!

And my pockets full, too! Huzza!

Cold Apple Soup with Raisins

In the world of fruit soups, apples offer rich texture and considerable versatility. This recipe draws its inspiration from a soup popular in Argentina, where apples are an important cash crop. Of course, no real gaucho would ever add the yogurt. Serve it as a light, refreshing first course to a meal of pork or roasted game, accompanied by a full-bodied dry hard cider or white wine.

4 large Jonathan, Stayman Winesap, Cortland, or other aromatic saucing apples, unpeeled, quartered, and cored

1 cup dry hard cider

1/2 cup golden raisins

2 eggs, separated

Salt

About 1 tablespoon sugar

1/2 cup chilled whole-milk plain yogurt, whisked until smooth

Paper-thin red apple slices rubbed with freshly squeezed lemon juice or minced fresh tarragon for garnish

Thin strips of lemon zest for garnish

Combine the apple quarters in a saucepan with just enough water to cover. Bring to a boil over medium-high heat, reduce the heat to medium-low, and simmer, uncovered, for 10 to 15 minutes, or until tender.

Remove from the heat and pass the contents of the pan through a food mill or sieve placed over a nonreactive saucepan. The purée should have the consistency of a thin applesauce. Add the cider and raisins and place over medium heat. Bring to a simmer and cook gently for about 5 minutes, or until the raisins are plump. At this point, the soup should have a creamy consistency. If it does not, stir in a little water to correct it. Remove from the heat.

In a small bowl, whisk the egg yolks until blended, then whisk in about 3/4 cup of the hot soup. Slowly whisk the egg mixture into the remaining hot soup. Add a dash of salt and the sugar to taste. Let cool, cover, and chill well.

Just before serving, in a medium-sized bowl, beat the egg whites until soft peaks form. Fold the yogurt into the egg whites, then fold the mixture into the chilled soup. Taste and adjust with salt and/or sugar.

Ladle into chilled bowls and garnish each serving with the apple slices or fresh tarragon and the lemon zest. Serve immediately.

SERVES 4 TO 6

Roasted Winter Squash Soup with Cider

Some flavors require frost. After Labor Day, we couldn't give peaches away. Before Independence Day, nobody would buy blackberries. It's the same with the rich, earthy winter squashes. I can't eat them when it's still sweaty weather, but come that first autumn cold snap, when scarlet begins to ink the maples, the craving begins. Dense acorns, creamy butternuts, buttery Delicatas, vaguely spicy turbans. As I child, I had them simply roasted, the halves laid upside down in a little water until tender, then flipped and a pat of butter and some brown sugar slipped into the hollows. Once I discovered the delights of hard cider cookery, I switched to soups, which can be meals in themselves. However you use the squashes, always begin by roasting them in the oven to bring out their own tawny sugars. —FB

1 butternut squash, about 2 pounds, or
2 Delicata squashes, about 1 pound each

1 bottle (750 ml) semisweet hard cider

2 thin slices peeled fresh ginger

2 or 3 fresh sage leaves

Salt

1 tablespoon sugar, or ¹/₂ cup fresh cider, if needed

¹/₂ to ²/₃ cup heavy cream

Freshly grated nutmeg

Paper-thin unpeeled apple rings sautéed in unsalted butter and small handful of fresh sage leaves (optional) for garnish

Preheat the oven to 375°F.

Cut the squash(es) in half lengthwise and scoop out and discard the seeds and fibers. Place the halves cut side down in a shallow baking pan and add water to a depth of ³/₈ inch. Roast for 35 to 45 minutes, or until tender, checking from time to time to be sure that the water does not cook away. Remove from the oven and let cool until they can be handled. Scoop out the flesh into a bowl. You should have about 2 cups. Press with a fork until smooth, then whip with the fork until creamy.

Transfer the squash purée to a heavy saucepan and add the hard cider, ginger, and sage leaves. Place over medium heat, bring to a simmer, and cook, uncovered, for 20 minutes, or until slightly reduced and the flavors have blended. Season with salt. If the soup seems a little starchy (squashes vary as to how starchy or sweet they are), add the sugar or fresh cider to sweeten it, then cook for 5 minutes longer.

Remove and discard the ginger slices and sage leaves. Pour in the cream, adding as much as is needed to create a nice consistency, and cook, stirring, for a few minutes to blend the flavors.

Ladle into warmed bowls. Top each serving with 2 or 3 gratings of nutmeg, then garnish each serving with 2 or 3 apple rings. Float a sage leaf in the center of each ring. Serve immediately.

SERVES 6

VARIATION: Substitute ¹/₂ cup plain whole-milk yogurt, whisked and at room temperature, for the cream. Omit the ginger and remove the soup from the heat before stirring in the yogurt.

Parsnip and Cider Soup

French chefs have been putting parsnips in their potages for centuries, but Americans tend to be chary of using these white, slightly woody underground treats. They're always a good addition to mashed potatoes. You can slice them and sauté them in butter and oil. Or you can make a splendid, hearty soup like this one that is at once rich and creamy, yet bright and tangy from the dried apples and cider.

2 pounds parsnips, peeled

Vegetable oil for oiling parsnips

2 tablespoons unsalted butter

1 leek, including about 2 inches of the pale green, chopped

1/3 cup chopped dried apples

3 to 4 cups chicken stock

1 1/2 cups dry or semidry hard cider

Salt

Freshly ground pepper

1/2 cup heavy cream

1 carrot, peeled and finely diced

4 or 5 fresh mint leaves, finely chopped

Chopped fresh mint for garnish

Preheat the oven to 350°F.

Rub the parsnips with the vegetable oil, wrap in aluminum foil, and place on a baking sheet. Roast for 35 to 40 minutes, or until nearly tender when pierced with a knife. (The parsnips can instead be boiled, but roasting produces a sweeter, more intense flavor.) Unwrap and, when cool enough to handle, cut into 1-inch lengths.

In a saucepan, melt 1 tablespoon of the butter over low heat. Add the leek, stir to coat with the butter, cover, and cook for 5 minutes, or until softened. Add the parsnips, dried apples, and 3 cups of the stock and raise the heat to medium. Bring to a simmer, adjust the heat to maintain a steady simmer, and cook, uncovered, for about 30 minutes, or until the apple pieces are plump and tender.

Working in batches, transfer the soup to a food processor and process until smooth. (Roasted parsnips tend to be too fibrous to pass through a food mill.) Return the purée to the saucepan and add the cider and enough additional stock to achieve a smooth, creamy consistency. Season with salt and pepper. Simmer gently for 20 minutes to blend the flavors. Stir in the cream and simmer gently for 10 minutes longer. Taste and adjust the seasonings.

While the soup is cooking, melt the remaining 1 tablespoon butter in a small frying pan. Add the carrot and finely chopped mint and sauté for a few minutes, or until the carrot is tender. Remove from the heat.

Ladle the soup into warmed bowls. Garnish each serving with the carrot and a little chopped mint. Serve immediately.

SERVES 6

Sea Scallops in Cider Sauce

Deprived of either the soil or the sun necessary for making fine wine, the Normans and the Bretons were forced into becoming gustatory contrarians in France. *Les fruits de mer* are their great pride. Add the great farmhouse beverage, *cidre*, fermented from very carefully blended selections of bitter-sharp and bitter-sweet cider apples, and seafood cookery takes on a color unavailable anywhere else in the world. Several summers, journalist and Sicilian chef nonpareil Frank Viviano and I spent a week exploring the cider culture of northern Brittany. Cider making first came to Brittany about twelve hundred years earlier, and traditional cooks never hesitated to blend the products of the sea with those of the land. Coquilles St. Jacques and *cidre* claimed a place on nearly every menu in the fishing villages along the Vallée de la Rance inland from St. Malo. This recipe is a variation on that bounty. A dry, somewhat musky French cider works best, but any good-quality one will do. —FB

1¹/₂ carrots, peeled and cut into 2¹/₂-inch lengths

2 tablespoons minced leek, a mixture of white and pale green

2 tablespoons minced yellow onion

Pinch of coarse sea salt

Bouquet garni of 4 sprigs flat-leaf parsley, 2 sprigs thyme, 1 bay leaf, 5 white peppercorns, and 5 pink peppercorns

2¹/₄ cups dry hard cider

32 sea scallops

6 tablespoons heavy cream

In a saucepan, combine the carrots, leek, onion, and salt. Place the ingredients of the bouquet garni on a square of cheesecloth, bring the corners together, and tie securely. Add to the saucepan along with the cider and place over high heat. Bring to a boil and cook, uncovered, for 10 minutes. Remove from the heat, remove and discard the bouquet garni, and strain the liquid through a fine-mesh sieve placed over a clean, wide saucepan. Reserve the onion, leek, and carrots.

Return the strained liquid to a boil. Add the scallops, decrease the heat to medium, and cook, turning the scallops at the halfway point, for about 2 minutes, or until just opaque throughout. Using a slotted spoon, transfer the scallops to a warmed platter; keep warm.

Add the reserved onion and leek to the liquid along with the cream and simmer over medium-high heat for a few minutes, or until thickened to a light, creamy consistency.

Meanwhile, cut the carrot pieces into long, slender julienne. Divide the scallops among 8 warmed individual plates and spoon the sauce over them. Decorate with the carrot julienne and serve immediately.

SERVES 8

Steamed Clams, Asturian Style

My friend Cecilia Brunazzi tagged along for another trek into the peculiar byways of ancient cider culture, this one through Asturias and Basque country, so-called Green Spain. The Asturians (who are mostly Gauls) and the Basques (whose origins no one knows) were fermenting apples well before the Romans pillaged their way west, and they will toss a glass of cider into almost anything they're cooking. On our first day out from Oviedo, the Asturian capital, we were looking for ruins of the circular stone fortifications at Coana, from which the old Gauls had fought off the Roman brigades. A coastline that makes Big Sur seem puppy tame distracted us, and we took a corkscrew road down to a bit of a fishing village called Cudillero. It was October, too chilly to sit outside, and all the tourists had gone home to London and Frankfurt, leaving the tables full of locals. We stepped into a nearly empty cafe with chalk-white walls and fish pictures all around.

"Clams and *fabada* beans cooked in cider?" I said to Cecilia.

Her silent smile told me I had to try it. Only after the foot-long ceramic dish arrived at the table, puffing fragrant clouds of garlic, apple, and sea before it, did she confess her newly developed shellfish allergy. They were all mine. Lucky me. By the time lunch was done, there wasn't enough left in the dish for the cat to lick.

Clams in cider, it turned out, were common along the coast, but only in the cafe in Cudillero were they simmered with the long, creamy *fabada* beans, another Asturian specialty hardly available in the rest of Spain, much less across the ocean. You could add cider-simmered cannellini beans to this dish, but it wouldn't be the same, and anyway the simpler cider and clams make elegant companions. (Oh, yes, we never made it to the ruins.) —FB

1¹/₂ tablespoons olive oil

2 cloves garlic, slivered

³/₄ cup dry hard cider

1 rounded teaspoon tomato paste

2 tablespoons chopped fresh flat-leaf parsley

16 littleneck or cherrystone clams, well scrubbed

In a frying pan, warm the olive oil over medium heat. Add the garlic and sauté for about 2 minutes, or until soft but not browned. Pour in the cider and stir in the tomato paste and 1 tablespoon of the parsley. Raise the heat to medium-high, bring to a boil, and add the clams, discarding any that do not close to the touch. Cover and cook, shaking the pan occasionally, for 3 to 5 minutes, or until the clams open.

(continued)

Using a slotted spoon, divide the clams between 2 individual bowls, discarding any that failed to open. Pour the cooking liquid over the top and garnish with the remaining 1 tablespoon parsley. Serve at once.

SERVES 2

Delta Crayfish in Hard Cider

Almost anything you do with California's San Joaquin Delta crayfish will be good so long as you don't overcook them. A quick boil is invariably delicious, but this version, an adaptation of a shrimp dish found along the Norman coast of France, adds a bright, lyrical fragrance to the already sweet, spiny creatures.

1 bottle (750 ml) semisweet hard cider

2 tablespoons coarse sea salt

3 pounds crayfish

Baguette slices and unsalted butter as an accompaniment

In a saucepan, bring the cider to a boil over high heat. Add the salt and crayfish. Boil for 8 to 10 minutes, or until the crayfish turn bright red.

Drain and transfer to a serving bowl. Serve immediately with the bread and butter.

SERVES 4

Monkfish Liver in Gingered Cider

Browning can never resist buying an offbeat food. Then he invariably rings me up to ask how to cook it.

"So, I was just at the farmers' market at Grand Army Plaza and I bought a monkfish liver," he announced one Saturday afternoon. "I have never eaten one before. What should I do with it?"

"Well, I love the stuff," I said, "but I've only ever had it in Japanese restaurants, served cold with *ponzu* sauce. It's rich and wonderful—a kind of poor woman's foie gras. But I haven't got a clue what you should do with it. Do you know any Japanese chefs?"

"Nope, not a one. But I do have some cider and . . ."

The recipe for this very classy first course showed up in my Sunday morning e-mail. —SS

$^{1}/_{2}$ **cup dry hard cider**

1 teaspoon peeled and finely chopped fresh ginger

1 teaspoon canola or other flavorless vegetable oil

1 monkfish liver, about $^{1}/_{3}$ pound

Salt

1$^{1}/_{2}$ teaspoons minced fresh flat-leaf parsley

4 thin slices sourdough bread, toasted and kept warm

Pour the cider into a small frying pan and add the ginger. Bring to a boil over medium-high heat, adjust the heat to maintain a vigorous simmer, and simmer for 1 minute to infuse the cider with the ginger.

Add the oil, then add the liver. Cook over medium-high heat for 1$^{1}/_{2}$ to 2 minutes, or until it browns on the first side. Turn and continue to cook for 1$^{1}/_{2}$ to 2 minutes more, or until it browns on the second side but is still very rosy inside. The timing will depend upon the thickness of the liver. Season with salt.

Transfer to a plate and pour the pan sauce over the top. (It will have become almost syrupy.) Sprinkle with the parsley. Cut into $^{1}/_{4}$-inch-thick slices and serve with the warm toast.

SERVES 2 TO 4

Duck and Apples in Puff Pastry

On one of my apple meanderings, two former San Franciscans, Robert Kramer, the expat American filmmaker, and his wife, Erica Asher, a masseuse whose kneading fingers define the divine, invited me to their converted country schoolhouse beside the Seine. I brought a new cider I wanted to taste. A neighbor appeared shortly after dusk with four salacious duck breasts, pink, plump, and freshly skinned. Dressed with nothing more than a sprinkle of salt and a bit of oil, we set them on a grate above the coals in the great Norman fireplace (it was big enough for two adults to sleep in). Never has a duck given more for its country. . . . But there were four breasts and only three of us. What to do? The next morning we came up with the following sinfully rich little invention, a variation on a traditional Norman specialty prepared with wild game. We used Reinettes, a beloved old French apple. Back in San Francisco, a Chinese roast duck purchased on Clement Street, in the so-called New Chinatown, proved an excellent shortcut. —FB

½ large **Chinese roast duck**

1 tablespoon **unsalted butter**

3 tablespoons **finely chopped yellow onion**

1 **Jonathan, Jonagold, or other sweet-tart apple, peeled, cored, and cut into** ¼-**inch dice**

Salt

Freshly ground white pepper

½ cup **heavy cream**

About 1 pound **puff pastry, thawed if frozen**

1 small **egg yolk, lightly beaten**

Skin and bone the roast duck half and chop the meat into ¼-inch dice. You should have about 1 cup. Set aside.

In a frying pan, melt the butter over medium heat. Add the onion and sauté for about 3 minutes, or until translucent. Add the duck and apple and continue to cook, stirring, until the apple just begins to soften, about

2 minutes. Season to taste with salt and white pepper. (The amount of salt you need will depend upon how highly seasoned the duck is. You may not need any at all.) Pour in the cream and cook, stirring occasionally, for about 5 minutes, or until the cream thickens and reduces. Taste and adjust the seasonings. Remove from the heat and let cool completely.

Preheat the oven to 400°F. On a lightly floured work surface, roll out the puff pastry about ⅛ inch thick. Cut into 4-inch squares. Divide the cooled filling evenly among the squares, placing it in the center. Brush a stripe of egg yolk along the edge of each square and fold the square in half to form a triangle, pressing the edges to seal securely. Place on an ungreased baking sheet.

Bake for about 20 minutes, or until the pastry is puffed and lightly golden. Serve immediately.

SERVES 8

MAIN DISHES

Braised Chicken, Norman Style

In the past, restaurateurs in Normandy automatically placed a bottle of hard cider on the table, the same way a carafe of water was—and still is—commonplace elsewhere in France. And, like the water, it never appeared on the bill. Alas, to our dismay, that civilized custom slipped out of fashion more than half a century ago. In tribute to a tradition abandoned too soon, we suggest you open a good dry Norman cider to sip along with this chicken.

6 chicken thighs

Salt

Freshly ground pepper

2 tablespoons unsalted butter

2 or 3 fresh sage leaves, or 2 pinches dried sage

About 1¹/₂ cups dry or semisweet hard cider, or as needed

¹/₂ cup heavy cream

2 tablespoons Calvados (optional)

Fresh sage leaves for garnish

Rinse the chicken thighs and pat dry. Sprinkle generously with salt and pepper.

In a heavy enameled casserole or deep frying pan over medium heat, melt the butter. Add the chicken thighs and brown well on both sides, about 10 minutes. Add the sage and pour in enough cider to cover all but the tops of the thighs. Bring to a simmer, decrease the heat to medium-low, and simmer, uncovered, for about 30 minutes, or until tender and opaque throughout when pierced with a knife.

Remove the thighs to a warmed platter and keep warm. Add the cream to the cooking liquid, raise the heat to high, and boil for 4 to 5 minutes, or until rich and creamy. Add the Calvados for the last 2 minutes of cooking. Taste and adjust the seasonings.

Spoon the sauce over the chicken thighs and garnish with the sage leaves. Serve at once.

SERVES 6

VARIATIONS:

- Add ¹/₄ cup finely diced Bayonne or other salt-cured ham when you brown the thighs.
- About 6 ounces fresh mushrooms such as chanterelle, cremini, or domestic white, sliced and sautéed in butter until tender, can be added with the Calvados.
- For a rich garnish, sauté unpeeled rings of Jonathan or eastern Golden Delicious apples in unsalted butter until golden, then flame with a little Calvados before strewing them over the finished dish.

Stuffed Chicken Thighs with Gruyère and Crème Fraîche

At one point during the writing of this book, our editor started us to worrying about calories and grams of fat, clogged arteries and high blood pressure, suggesting that most people were not ready for so many recipes that guaranteed the stock portfolios of family doctors. We both grew up in a world of slab bacon and fresh dairy cream, but, like nearly all boomers, we have also both reached the point in our lives when we think twice about the skin on our poultry and the butter on our bread. So when we received a recipe from a French chef who tucked cholesterol-carrying bacon as well as healthy apple slices into a poultry-thigh pocket, and then heaped on considerably more crème fraîche and Gruyère than you see here, we decided to create this "lite" version.

4 boneless, skinless chicken thighs, about 5 ounces each

Salt

Freshly ground pepper

3 tablespoons unsalted butter

4 unpeeled wedges from a Jonathan, Jonagold, or Braeburn apple, each about 3/8 inch thick

4 slices from a fresh portobello mushroom, each about 3/8 inch thick

3/4 cup crème fraîche (see note)

1/4 cup finely shredded Gruyère cheese

Rinse the chicken thighs and pat dry. Cut a horizontal pocket in each thigh about 2 inches long and three-fourths of the way through. Season the pockets and the outsides of the thighs with salt and pepper.

Position a rack in the upper third of the oven and pre-heat to 500°F.

In a large sauté pan, melt 1 tablespoon of the butter over medium-high heat. Add the apple wedges and sauté, turning as needed, for about 5 minutes, or until golden brown and tender. Transfer to a plate.

Add another tablespoon of the butter to the same pan over medium-high heat. When it melts, add the mushroom slices and sauté for 8 to 10 minutes, or until tender. Season with salt and pepper and remove from the heat.

Slip an apple wedge and a mushroom slice into the pocket in each thigh and secure closed with toothpicks. Melt the remaining 1 tablespoon butter in the same pan over medium-high heat. Add the chicken and cook, turning once, for 12 to 15 minutes, or until well browned on both sides and opaque throughout.

Transfer the stuffed thighs to a baking dish and spoon the crème fraîche around them. Sprinkle the Gruyère cheese evenly over the tops of the thighs. Bake for 2 to 3 minutes, or until the cheese melts and begins to brown.

Remove from the oven and serve the chicken with the sauce created by the crème fraîche.

SERVES 4

NOTE: If you don't have crème fraîche on hand and can't find it at the corner store, mix 1 tablespoon sour cream into 3/4 cup heavy cream in a glass, place it on a trivet in a bowl, and add warm water to the bowl to reach about two-thirds up the sides of the glass. Set the bowl atop the living room steam radiator or gas space heater or in an oven with a pilot light. Leave it overnight. A yogurt maker would work, too, and so perhaps would a baby-bottle warmer. An even quicker method is to mix together 1/2 cup sour cream and 1/4 cup half-and-half and let the mixture stand at room temperature for 30 to 60 minutes.

Paleobotanists believe that apples, which have seventeen pairs of chromosomes, are a cross of two other plants: a primitive plum of the *Rosaceae* family that has eight pairs of chromosomes and a white-and-yellow flower of the *Spiraea* genus called meadowsweet that has nine pairs.

BRAEBURN

Chicken Breasts with Cider, Spices, and Caramelized Apples

Daniel Orr grew up on a farm across the Ohio River from Kentucky and up a ways into Indiana. We Kentuckians tend to look down our crooked country noses at Midwesterners, especially when it comes to what we think of as their pasty Yankee kitchens. Hard as it is to confess, we've surely got it wrong when it comes to this Hoosier country boy, who made a name for himself by bringing wit, imagination, and irresistible new recipes first to New York's most classic traditional French restaurant, La Grenouille, where he was executive chef in the mid-1990s, and later to the city's famed Guastavino's.

Spices are Daniel's passion. He thinks of them as perfume for the palate, which has led him to grind, blend, and market his own Daniel Orr's Kitchen d'Orr Spice Blends. He uses his New Regime Spice Blend (which includes, among other things, coriander, mustard, star anise, and nutmeg) on meats, fish, vegetables, rice, and fruits. If you can't find it at your local gourmet shop or can't wait for a mail-order delivery (*www.chef-daniel-orr.com*), substitute sharper-flavored five-spice powder. —FB

¹/₄ cup dark raisins

¹/₄ cup golden raisins

¹/₂ cup Madeira or port

¹/₂ cup hot water

6 boneless chicken breast halves with skin intact

2 tablespoons New Regime Spice Blend (see recipe introduction), or 1 tablespoon five-spice powder

2 teaspoons coarse sea salt, plus salt to taste

Freshly ground pepper

3 tablespoons clarified unsalted butter

3 Granny Smith apples, peeled with peels reserved, cored, and cut lengthwise into eighths

2 tablespoons all-purpose flour

³/₄ cup cider vinegar

2 cups brown chicken stock (see note)

¹/₄ cup unsalted butter

¹/₄ cup honey

Juice of ¹/₂ lemon

2 tablespoons chopped fresh flat-leaf Italian parsley for garnish

1 tablespoon candied orange peel for garnish

In a small bowl, combine the dark and golden raisins, wine, and hot water and let stand for 3 to 4 hours, or until the raisins are fully plumped.

Preheat the oven to 450°F.

Season the chicken breasts with 1 tablespoon of the Regime blend or 1¹/₂ teaspoons of the five-spice powder, the 2 teaspoons salt, and pepper to taste.

In a large, ovenproof sauté pan, heat the clarified butter over medium-high heat. Place the chicken breasts, skin side down, in the pan and cook for about 5 minutes, or until well browned and most of the fat has cooked out of the skin. Turn the breasts over and sear the other side for about 3 minutes. Pour off any excess fat.

Add the apple peels to the pan, slipping them under the chicken breasts. Place the pan in the oven and bake for 8 to 10 minutes, or until the chicken breasts are opaque throughout. Transfer the breasts to a warmed serving platter and cover to keep warm. Leave the apple peels in the pan.

Dust the apple peels with the flour. Cook over medium heat, stirring often, for about 5 minutes. Pour in the vinegar and deglaze the pan, stirring to dislodge any bits stuck to the pan bottom. Cook until the liquid is reduced by half. Pour in the stock, bring to a boil, and decrease the heat to medium so the liquid simmers gently.

In another sauté pan, melt 3 tablespoons of the unsalted butter over medium-high heat until the butter is brown and smells toasty. Do not allow it to burn. Add the apples, honey, lemon juice, and the remaining 1 tablespoon Regime blend or 1$1/2$ teaspoons five-spice powder. Sauté the apples, turning them as needed, for 5 to 8 minutes, or until they are a rich, even brown and are tender. Season with pepper.

Pour any juice released from the chicken into the pan with the apples. Arrange the chicken on the platter and top with the caramelized apples. Drain off any liquid from the raisins and sprinkle the raisins on top.

Add the remaining 1 tablespoon unsalted butter to the pan with the simmering liquid and stir until melted. Season to taste with salt and pepper. Pour the sauce through a fine-mesh sieve over the chicken and apples. Garnish with the parsley and candied orange peel.

SERVES 6

NOTE: Brown stock is a rich stock made by roasting chicken parts or bones and vegetables before they are cooked in liquid.

Petaluma Creek Roasted Chicken

When I was a kid, chickens pretty much meant only one thing to me: work. That meant feeding them, gathering and then buffing up their eggs for sale to the Petaluma co-op, and gutting, plucking, and singeing them after someone else, ax in hand, had delivered them up for the table. The big, old birds served for those distant Sunday suppers were a far cry from the young, plump, free-range babes I buy today. The residents of our old-fashioned chicken yard were, by default, free-range, and they did enjoy a sound diet that included clippings from a kale patch my grandfather sowed especially for them. But once they became pensioners—their last eggs laid—they were candidates for the kitchen, and then, in the spirit of frugality, we were encouraged to eat every part of the aged fowl. (As a result, I still love chicken feet today, snatching them off fast-rolling dim sum carts whenever I can.) Although this curiously fussy but delicious recipe was never part of my childhood, it does call for a big bird raised on a healthful diet and, ideally, dried apples from Browning Orchard. —SS

STUFFING

1/2 cup dried apples

3 tablespoons golden raisins or currants

1/2 cup semidry hard or fresh cider

1/4 cup unsalted butter

1 large yellow onion, chopped

1/2 celery stalk, thinly sliced (optional)

2/3 cup long-grain white rice

6 tablespoons almonds, toasted and finely chopped

1/2 teaspoon ground cardamom

1/4 teaspoon salt, or more salt to taste

About 1/3 cup finely chopped fresh flat-leaf parsley

• • • • •

1 free-range roasting chicken, about 6 pounds

Salt

Freshly ground pepper

1/4 cup unsalted butter

Semidry hard or fresh cider

3 tablespoons honey

1/2 teaspoon ground cardamom

To make the stuffing, in a small saucepan, combine the dried apples, raisins, and cider. Bring to a gentle simmer and cook for 10 to 15 minutes, or until the fruit is plumped. Drain, reserving any liquid. Chop the apples finely and, if using raisins, chop them as well. Set aside.

In a saucepan, melt the butter over medium heat. Add the onion and celery and sauté for about 8 minutes, or until tender. Add the rice and almonds and stir for about 3 minutes, or until the rice kernels are hot and well coated with the butter. Add the apples, raisins, cardamom, salt, and 1⅓ cups water. Raise the heat to medium-high and bring to a boil. Cover, reduce the heat to low, and cook for about 15 minutes, or until the liquid is absorbed. Remove from the heat and let cool to room temperature. Add the chopped parsley, tossing to mix. Taste and adjust the seasoning with salt.

Preheat the oven to 425°F.

To stuff and roast the chicken, rinse the chicken inside and out and pat dry. Season generously inside and out with salt and pepper. Spoon the rice stuffing into the cavity, being careful not to pack too fully. Truss the bird closed with kitchen string. Spoon any remaining stuffing into a small baking dish, cover with aluminum foil, and set aside.

Place the bird, breast side up, in a roasting pan. In a small saucepan, melt the butter over low heat. Measure the reserved liquid from the stuffing and add additional cider to equal ¼ cup. Add to the butter along with the honey and the cardamom. Brush some of the mixture onto the chicken.

Settlement requirements in the Ohio territories during the 1780s included a stipulation that farmers plant "at least fifty apple or pear trees and twenty peach trees" in order to secure a land deed.

Roast the chicken for about 20 minutes. Decrease the heat to 375°F and continue roasting, basting every 20 minutes or so with the honey mixture, for about 1½ hours, or until the juices run clear when a thigh is pierced. Place the baking dish containing the stuffing in the oven for the last 20 minutes or so of roasting, just to heat it through. If the bird begins to brown too much because of the honey in the basting mixture, cover the breast with aluminum foil.

When the chicken is ready, transfer it to a platter, cover loosely with foil, and let rest for about 10 minutes. Remove the separate dish of stuffing at the same time.

Snip the trussing string and spoon the stuffing into a warmed bowl, then add the stuffing from the baking dish to it. Carve the chicken and serve with the stuffing.

SERVES 4 TO 6

Baltic Roasted Goose with Sour Apples

Goose hunting for the feasts of the winter solstice seems to be an almost primal association for the stout folk who have long tended the fields and forests of the north. Before gunpowder brought firearms to the West, capturing the wild goose or pheasant fell to the wily trapper or the sharp-eyed archer. Those wild, gamy birds required a good deal more attention than the ones we pick up at the butcher. One standard French country technique calls for curing the feathered fowl by hanging it from a hook in the meat house for at least three days or, as described in the words of the official text published in 1900 by the Cordon Bleu cooking school, *"jusqu'il a commencé à décomposer."* After the meat was softened in this way, there was, of course, still more to do. Rubbing the inside of the bird with caraway seeds has remained common in Russia, Scandinavia, and the Baltic countries and in Jewish cookery. Adding chopped sour wild apples probably dates to an even earlier era, back to the time of the mischief-making Loki, who threatened his fellow Nordic gods by conspiring with the evil giants to steal the apples of immortality.

1 goose, about 12 pounds

Coarse sea salt

Freshly ground pepper

2 teaspoons dried marjoram, crumbled

$1/2$ teaspoon caraway seeds

4 Granny Smith, Newtown Pippin, Jonathan, or other tart apples, unpeeled, cored, and cut into $1/2$-inch cubes

Boiling water as needed

Marjoram or flat-leaf parsley sprigs for garnish

Preheat the oven to 400°F.

Rinse the goose inside and out, then pat dry. With fork tines, prick the skin of the bird along the lower breast, on the thighs, and across the back. Season the outside generously with coarse salt and pepper, then sprinkle the cavity with the marjoram and caraway seeds and rub them into the cavity walls. Pack the apples into the cavity and truss closed with trussing needles or kitchen string. Place the goose, breast side up, on a rack in a large roasting pan, tucking the wing tips beneath the body.

Roast for about 20 minutes. Decrease the heat to 350°F and continue to roast, basting the goose with $1/4$ cup boiling water every 20 to 25 minutes, for about $2 1/4$ hours longer. To test for doneness, insert an instant-read thermometer in the thickest part of the thigh, away from the bone; it should read 170°F. Alternatively, pierce the thigh with the tip of a sharp knife; the juices should run clear.

Transfer the bird to a large platter. Cover loosely with aluminum foil and let rest for 15 minutes before carving.

When ready to serve, remove the trussing needles or snip the string and spoon the apples into a warmed serving bowl. Decorate the platter with marjoram. Carve the goose at the table.

SERVES 8

Turkey Breast Tagine with Apples

It was Christmas Eve 1970, and my friend Walter and I, then resident in a dusty VW bus for some four months, rolled into Agadir, on Morocco's Atlantic seaboard. A spate of engine trouble had kept us from fully enjoying the hundred-mile drive from Essaouira, although I can still remember the picture-postcard last leg, with the purple mountains on our left and the deep blue sea on our right. Our final destination, still distant and a few days off, was the walled settlement of Goulimine, site of the last camel market (the source of much-beloved hippie beads) before the Sahara, a journey described as treacherous by folks who had braved it.

We settled in at the local campground and then, discovering that an enterprising fellow camper had arranged for a Christmas meal, joined a long, slow motor caravan of some twenty holiday-dinner seekers, finally pulling up in front of a two-story building surrounded only by the inky night. We entered and were signaled upstairs, passing a dozen or so djellaba-clad Moroccan men on the first floor, their hookahs stoked, staring blankly at a single television set broadcasting—believe me—an old Bugs Bunny cartoon. Upstairs, a long wooden table, fully set, awaited us. A row of low-slung earthenware pots with high conical lids, alternating with vessels of couscous, stretched its length. Each high-rise container, called a *tagine slaoui*, concealed a whole chestnut-brown turkey surrounded with fresh and dried fruits. The circular lids lifted, we consumed the contents, and then we capped off the meal with honey-drenched pastries, sweet mint tea, and, for interested parties, a few hits off of one of the hookahs provided by the management but stocked by the celebrants.

Admittedly, this is not the holiday dish served on that memorable Moroccan Christmas, which is what most cookbook authors would offer at this point in the story. But it is a first-rate main course, rich with the flavors of North Africa, that does justice to a Christmas Eve to remember. Don't forget the couscous. —SS

¼ cup plus 3 tablespoons unsalted butter

1½ teaspoons ground ginger

1 teaspoon salt

1 teaspoon freshly ground black pepper

¼ to ½ teaspoon saffron threads

4 small dried red chiles, or ½ teaspoon cayenne pepper

1 boneless, skinless turkey breast, 3½ to 4 pounds, tied

2 yellow onions, chopped

½ cup chopped fresh cilantro, plus sprigs for garnish

2 cinnamon sticks, each 4 inches long

About 2 cups chicken stock

3 Granny Smith, Newtown Pippin, or other tart green apples, peeled, halved, cored, and thinly sliced lengthwise

1 to 2 teaspoons ground cinnamon

1 tablespoon superfine sugar

In a Dutch oven or other large, heavy pot, melt ¼ cup of the butter over medium heat. Add the ginger, salt, pepper, saffron, and chiles, stir for 10 to 15 seconds to release the flavors, and add the turkey breast. Turn to coat it evenly with the butter and spices. Scatter the onions and chopped cilantro around the breast, add the cinnamon sticks, and then pour in enough stock to reach about halfway up the sides of the breast. Increase the heat to medium-high, bring to a simmer, cover, decrease the heat to low, and cook, turning the breast over every 15 minutes or so, for 45 to 60 minutes, or until an instant-read thermometer inserted into the thickest part of the breast registers 145°F. Do not over-cook the meat at this point, or it will be dry.

Transfer the breast to a platter. Raise the heat to high under the cooking liquid and boil for about 10 minutes, or until reduced by about half. Discard the cinnamon sticks and taste and adjust the seasonings.

Meanwhile, melt the remaining 3 tablespoons butter in a frying pan over medium-high heat. Working in batches, add the apple slices, sprinkle with some of the ground cinnamon and sugar, and sauté, turning once, for 5 to 10 minutes, or until nicely golden and caramelized.

Snip the strings on the turkey breast and cut into ¼-inch-thick slices. Arrange the apple slices around the edges of the platter and pour the reduced pan juices over the meat. Garnish with cilantro sprigs and serve immediately.

SERVES 8

Duck Legs and Pink Ladies

Sometimes an idea floats into your mind like a mallard onto a pond. Here we were after we finished our Duck Breast and Fuji Apples on Watercress (page 41) wondering what to do with these fine duck legs that would have been the envy of a quacking Jane Powell or Cyd Charisse. Browning had been raving on about the wonderful new apple from Australia called Pink Lady, when a saucy idea slipped into Silva's nouvelle California head. Why not marry the two? If it tastes as good as it looks on the page, maybe we could write a musical farce called *The Duck Legs & Pink Ladies Review*. Several rehearsals later, we gave up on the theater piece but decided, with all due credit to the guesthouse kitchens we'd visited in Normandy and to the apple breeders Down Under, to keep the recipe. And yes, the thighs are good, too.

4 duck legs, 1/2 to 3/4 pound each, trimmed of visible fat

Salt

Freshly ground pepper

1 1/2 teaspoons dried thyme

2 tablespoons unsalted butter

1 tablespoon olive oil

12 to 16 small white onions, each 3/4 to 1 inch in diameter

2 turnips, about 1 pound total, peeled and cut lengthwise into sixths

2 teaspoons superfine sugar

3 Pink Lady, Jonagold, or other sweet-tart apples, about 1 1/2 pounds total, peeled, cored, and cut lengthwise into sixths

1 cup semisweet hard cider

1 to 1 1/2 tablespoons Calvados or applejack

Finely chopped fresh flat-leaf parsley for garnish

Rinse the duck legs and pat dry. Season generously with salt, pepper, and thyme. Set aside.

Preheat the oven to 425°F.

In a large frying pan, melt 1 tablespoon of the butter with the olive oil over medium heat. Add the onions and sauté, turning as needed, for 5 to 10 minutes, or until browned on all sides but still firm. Using a slotted spoon, transfer to a baking dish large enough to accommodate the duck legs and other ingredients.

Return the pan to medium heat, add the turnips, and sprinkle with about 1 teaspoon of the sugar. Sauté, turning as needed, for 5 to 10 minutes, or until browned on all sides but still firm (the sugar hastens the browning). Using the slotted spoon, transfer them to the baking dish holding the onions.

Add the remaining 1 tablespoon butter to the pan over medium heat. When it melts, add the apple pieces, sprinkle with the remaining 1 teaspoon sugar, and sauté, turning as needed, for about 5 minutes, or until browned but still firm. Using the slotted spoon, transfer them to the baking dish.

Raise the heat to medium-high and add the duck legs, skin side down. Cook for 3 to 5 minutes, or until nicely browned. Add to the baking dish. Pour the cider into the pan and deglaze the pan over medium-high heat, stirring to dislodge any bits stuck to the pan bottom. Pour into the baking dish.

Bake for about 1 hour, or until the duck is tender when cut into with a knife and the vegetables and apples are tender when pierced with a fork. Using tongs or the slotted spoon, transfer the duck legs, apples, and vegetables to a warmed platter.

Pour the dish juices into a small saucepan, place over medium-high heat, add the Calvados, and cook for a few minutes until thickened slightly to a sauce consistency. Taste and adjust the seasonings with salt and pepper.

Pour the sauce over the duck and sprinkle the vegetables and duck with parsley. Serve at once.

SERVES 4

From the Delaware *News and Advertiser*, circa 1900:

Sussex County apple-jack—
Fill the jug, and hurry back;
Whether sick er well I be,
That's the medicine for me.
In the Winter, then she's prime,
Cools me off in summer-time;
She's a-comin, clear the track,—
Sussex County apple-jack!

Atlantic Salmon Fillets in Cider-Mustard Sauce

Mustard and cream might sound like an odd couple, but baked together on the back of a salmon fillet they make a handsome marriage. This recipe emerged one winter afternoon in Maysville, Kentucky, when the fish manager of the local Kroger chain waved me over to his counter. Knowing how pushy I was on the fish delivery dates, he assured me that the truck bearing these pert little fillets was still in the back lot, and he'd never have fresher ones. Once I got home, I loaded up the newly rebuilt fireplace with hickory and apple logs and called Silva out in San Francisco.

"So I've got a guest for dinner and these two succulent pieces of salmon," I said.

"Hmm," she said. "From the supermarket chain?"

"Yes, but really..." I tried to answer.

"Better make sure to add some hearty seasoning," she suggested. "Is he a new friend?"

"Honestly," I told her, "they're as fresh and frisky as anything at your self-consciously gourmet Monterey Market."

"Well, several years ago on a visit to Mont-Saint-Michel, I had lunch on the coast and the kitchen served a fine salmon coated with mustard in a little cream sauce."

"What kind of mustard? Just cream?"

"Grainy, country mustard, I think. And probably white wine for the braising liquid."

"Don't have any white wine out here and I can't get any. Anyway, you sure they didn't use cider?"

"Maybe. Could have been. Good heavens, that was twenty years ago!"

Now I'm sure cider was the right answer, for it perfectly bound the sweetness of the cream to the bite of the mustard seed. Alas, I panicked momentarily as I watched the cream begin to curdle when I poured it into the hot, acidic cider. But by the time the salmon emerged from the oven, the sauces had blended perfectly. And my guest couldn't have been happier. —FB

4 salmon fillets, each about 6 ounces and 1½ inches thick

Salt

About ½ cup whole-grain Dijon mustard

About 1 cup dry hard cider

⅓ cup heavy cream

Apple slices for garnish

Flat-leaf parsley sprigs for garnish

Position a rack in the upper third of the oven and preheat to 450°F.

Sprinkle the salmon fillets lightly with salt and arrange in a single layer in a baking pan. Spread the mustard thickly on the tops of the fillets. Pour the cider into the dish to a depth of about ¼ inch.

Bake for 10 minutes. Add the cream to the dish, return to the oven, and bake for 3 minutes. Baste the salmon with the cider-cream mixture and continue to bake for 2 minutes longer, or until the fish is just opaque throughout.

Transfer the fillets to warmed individual plates. If the mixture in the pan is too thin, place it on the stove top over medium-high heat and simmer to reduce and thicken slightly. Spoon over the fillets and serve garnished with apple slices and parsley.

SERVES 4

Oven-Braised Turbot in Cider and Cream

The trick to Norman cider cuisine, the proprietress of a guesthouse outside Dinan told me, is to use elemental ingredients grown in good Norman soil. Then she told me where to go for dinner and how to order: Avoid the dishes with complicated sauces and too many spices. True Norman chefs don't cook that way. Cider, fruit, butter, cream, frequently mushrooms. Subtle seasoning. Her sound advice is what led me to a sublime baked sole with cider, wild mushrooms, and cream. In this version, turbot stands in for the sole, since genuine day-old Dover sole is nearly impossible to find, and if you do find it, skinning it at home could prove daunting. The turbot fillets respond as though they were born to swim in cider. —FB

1½ large shallots, finely chopped

½ pound fresh oyster or cremini mushrooms, coarsely chopped

6 turbot or red snapper fillets, each about 6 ounces and 1½ inches thick

Salt

Freshly ground pepper

1½ cups dry hard cider, or more as needed

⅓ cup heavy cream

2 tablespoons unsalted butter, cut into bits

Preheat the oven to 400°F. Butter an attractive baking dish large enough to hold the fillets in a single layer.

Sprinkle half each of the shallots and mushrooms evenly over the bottom of the baking dish. Place the fish fillets on top and season with salt and pepper. Sprinkle the remaining shallots and mushrooms over the fillets. Stir together the cider and the cream and pour over the fish. The liquid should reach about three-fourths up the sides of the fillets. If the liquid is too shallow, add more cider as needed. Dot the fish with the butter.

Bake for about 20 minutes, or until the fish is opaque throughout and the sauce has thickened. Serve directly from the dish.

If the sauce remains too thin but the fish is cooked, remove the fillets from the baking dish to a warmed platter or individual plates. If you have used a flame-proof baking dish, place it on the stove top over medium-high heat and cook until reduced to a nice sauce consistency. If the dish is not flameproof, transfer its contents to a small saucepan and reduce. Spoon the sauce over the fish.

SERVES 6

Pascal's Rabbit

Chef Pascal Giraudeau grew up in La Rochelle, south of France's cider-apple orchards. Even after he moved to Paris, he never forgot the sharp fizz and tingle that cider brings to the thirsty palate, and he was always eager to add a bit of the bubbly elixir to his country's most traditional dishes. For several years he ran a couple of home-cookery restaurants near the Place de la Contrescarpe, where nearly a century ago Ernest Hemingway pounded out novels in an unheated, cold-water flat still marked by a street-level plaque. Although you can no longer savor Pascal's treats in the Contrescarpe neighborhood, you can easily cook up your own versions following his well-thought-out Old World dishes, including his *boudin noir aux pommes* (page 79), *tarte Tatin* (page 116), or this simple *lapin* dish.

3 tablespoons unsalted butter

1 tablespoon olive oil

1 rabbit, about 3½ pounds, cut into serving pieces

¾ cup finely chopped yellow onion

¾ cup peeled and finely chopped carrot

5 tablespoons all-purpose flour

2 cups dry or semidry hard cider

Salt

Freshly ground pepper

4 Newtown Pippin, Jonathan, Granny Smith, or other tart apples, peeled, cored, and cut into 1- to 1½-inch chunks

In a large sauté pan, melt the butter with the olive oil over medium-high heat. Add the rabbit pieces and brown on all sides, about 10 minutes. Transfer to a plate.

Decrease the heat to medium and add the onion and carrot to the fat remaining in the pan. Sauté for about 5 minutes, or until the onion is translucent. Stir in the flour until well mixed and cook, stirring, for a minute or two to rid it of its raw taste. Then slowly pour in the cider, stirring constantly. Cook over medium heat for 5 minutes to reduce slightly.

Return the browned rabbit to the pan and add water as needed just to cover the rabbit. Season with salt and pepper, bring to a simmer, and adjust the heat to maintain a gentle simmer. Cook, uncovered, for about 40 minutes, or until the rabbit is nearly tender.

Add the apples, distributing them evenly, and continue to cook gently for about 20 minutes, or until the apples and rabbit are tender to the tip of a knife.

Taste and adjust the seasoning. Transfer to a warmed serving dish and serve immediately.

SERVES 4

Pork Loin Stuffed with Fresh and Dried Apples

In her 1828 American volume *Directions for Cookery*, author Eliza Leslie took the notion of cooking from scratch seriously. She begins her pork roast instructions by calling for a "newly killed" pig. She meant it, too, advising further that, if at all possible, the beast should be slaughtered on the morning the roast was slated for the midday table. That didn't leave much time, so the home cook or, at best, her husband, was clearly expected to act as butcher. Today, many of us are too lazy (or don't even know how) to bone a pork loin, much less cut up the whole animal. If you fall into that category, ask the butcher to separate the bone from the loin and to butterfly the loin, leaving you only to assemble the easy triple-apple—fresh, dried, and cider—stuffing, lash it securely in the roast, and slip the whole works into the oven. Then you can put your feet up, pour a glass of cider, and get lost in a good novel until the loin is done, remembering that your nineteenth-century counterpart would still be at work carving up the rest of the pig.

STUFFING

2 tablespoons olive oil

1¹/₂ cups finely chopped yellow onion

2 cloves garlic, minced

1 tablespoon peeled and minced fresh ginger

2 Granny Smith, Newtown Pippin, or other tart green apples, peeled, cored, and chopped

1 cup chopped dried apples

3 tablespoons dried currants

1 tablespoon finely chopped fresh sage

1 cup dry hard cider

Salt

Freshly ground pepper

• • • • •

1 boneless pork loin, 4 to 5 pounds, butterflied

Coarse sea salt

Freshly ground pepper

About 6 sprigs sage

To make the stuffing, warm the olive oil in a large frying pan over medium heat. Add the onion, garlic, and ginger and sauté for about 5 minutes, or until the onion is translucent.

Add the fresh apples and sauté for 3 to 5 minutes, or until they begin to take on color. Add the dried apples, currants, and chopped sage and stir well. Pour in the cider, raise the heat to medium-high, and cook, stirring occasionally, until the cider is absorbed, about 5 minutes. Season with salt and pepper, remove from the heat, and let cool for about 10 minutes.

Meanwhile, preheat the oven to 400°F.

To stuff and roast the pork loin, lay the pork loin flat on a work surface and spread the cooled stuffing evenly over the meat. Roll up the loin into its original shape and, using kitchen string, tie at even intervals, pushing back any stuffing that tries to escape from the ends. Season the loin with coarse salt and pepper and tuck the sage sprigs under the strings. Place in a roasting pan.

Roast for about 1½ hours, until the meat is pale pink when the loin is cut into at the thickest point or an instant-read thermometer inserted into the thickest point registers 145°F to 150°F.

Transfer the pork loin to a cutting board and let stand for about 10 minutes before carving, then snip the strings and cut into slices. Arrange on a warmed platter and serve with Fox Mountain Parsnips (page 105).

SERVES 8

Baked Pork Chops Bayeux

Some years ago I took a train from Paris to Bayeux to see the Norman town's famous tapestry (an embroidery, really), *La Telle du Conquest*, an elaborate fifty-eight-scene depiction of the 1066 Norman conquest of England. Then, as now, Bayeux had considerable charms beyond its celebrated artwork, including a thriving lace industry; the big, beautiful eighteenth-century Lion d'Or hotel; and, as is the case with nearly every French town, some fine little bistros. I took my lunch in one of them, ordering a homey and delicious *plat du jour* that balanced an apple ring atop a thick pork chop sitting in a shallow pool of rich Norman cream. I followed it with a modest wedge of apple tart and a short, flared glass of the local Calvados. This recipe is a distant echo of that simple all-apple lunch. —SS

4 pork loin chops, each about 5 ounces
and 1 inch thick

Salt

Freshly ground pepper

1 1/2 teaspoons dried thyme or winter savory

2 tablespoons unsalted butter

2 tablespoons fine dried bread crumbs

1 large Granny Smith apple, unpeeled, cored
and sliced into 4 rings

1/2 to 3/4 cup heavy cream

Thyme sprigs for garnish

Preheat the oven to 450°F. Butter a baking dish in which the chops will fit snugly in a single layer.

Trim any excess fat from the chops. Season generously on both sides with salt and pepper and 1 1/4 teaspoons of the thyme.

In a frying pan, melt 1 tablespoon of the butter over medium-high heat. Add the chops and cook, turning once, for about 3 minutes total, or until well browned on both sides. Transfer to the prepared baking dish. Sprinkle the bread crumbs evenly over the tops of the chops.

In the same frying pan over medium heat, melt the remaining 1 tablespoon butter. Add the apple rings and cook, turning once, for about 5 minutes, or until they begin to take on color and soften slightly. Place a ring on top of each chop. Add the cream to the frying pan, bring to a simmer, and deglaze the pan, scraping up any browned bits from the pan bottom. Pour the cream evenly over the chops and dust with the remaining 1/4 teaspoon thyme.

Place in the oven and bake for 10 to 12 minutes, or until the chops are just cooked through and the apples are tender. Transfer to warmed individual plates and spoon the juices from the dish over the top. Garnish with thyme sprigs. Serve at once.

SERVES 4

Boudin Noir aux Pommes

Part of the charm of Pascal Giraudeau's restaurants (see page 75) was the simplicity of his menu. One clammy winter day I stopped in at his spot at 8 rue Tournefort and was presented with a double treat: this splendid mixture of roasted apples and blood sausage, which holds a primal place in the ancient French palate, and a modern story to match. It seems that the building housing Chez Pascal was a heroic address for the French Resistance during World War II. The 1940s proprietors would entertain German officers upstairs, feeding them spirits and wine to extract as much information as they could, while downstairs they hid downed English and American airmen. There's even a commemorative plaque on the door.

For those who are a bit squeamish about blood sausage (a rich, sweet treat among sausages, but hard to find in the United States), French or Louisiana *boudin blanc* or even bratwurst makes an acceptable compromise. Pascal also served slices of the *boudin noir* and apples on a crunchy salad of frisée as a first course. And now and then he would roast slices of small sweet potatoes with the apples and sausage for a dish he called *boudin noir aux deux pommes*. —FB

1¹/₂ tablespoons unsalted butter

2 teaspoons olive oil

2 boudins noirs, about 6 ounces each

2 Fuji, Jonagold, Jonathan, or other aromatic, firm apples, peeled, halved, cored, and sliced lengthwise

Preheat the oven to 400°F.

Place the butter and olive oil in a large ovenproof sauté pan and slip it into the oven just until the butter melts. Prick the sausages in several places with the tines of a fork and place in the pan. Arrange the sliced apples alongside. Return the pan to the oven and bake, turning the sausages and apples once at the halfway point, for about 20 minutes, or until the apples are tender and the sausages are slightly crisp on the outside and heated through.

Divide the sausages and apples between 2 warmed dinner plates, arranging the apple slices in a fan, and serve at once.

SERVES 2

Saturday Night Supper of Fried Apples, Sausage, and Biscuits

··

Two basic memories stand out about Saturday nights in the 1950s: Lawrence Welk on black-and-white TV, pressing his stubby fingers into his accordion and leading the band with "a one and a two and a . . .," preceded by a supper of fried apples and sausage at the kitchen table. Were I to refine the memory, I'd have to say that those Saturday nights must have come in the fall, when the Goldens and the Jonathans—without dissent the all-time best frying-apple mixture—were in. Aside from the fact that it tasted so good, it was one of the simplest and easiest meals to make during apple harvest, a season that for growers everywhere is kind of like an annual horticultural D-day. To today's cooks, biscuits might seem like a big deal, but in my parents' generation they were ordinary. They took only about five minutes to make and ten or twelve to cook. What's more, as leftovers, they also took care of Sunday morning breakfast. One more point: unstylish and nostalgic as it is, I still slice up wedges of iceberg lettuce, crosscut them, and pour on a spicy, homemade Russian dressing to serve alongside the sausage and apples. —FB

BISCUITS

2 cups all-purpose flour

1 tablespoon baking powder

³/₄ teaspoon salt

¹/₄ cup solid vegetable shortening

³/₄ cup milk

• • • • •

3 tablespoons unsalted butter

4 apples of at least two varieties, such as eastern Golden Delicious, Jonathan, Pink Lady, Stayman Winesap, or Jonagold, unpeeled, halved, cored, and cut lengthwise into ³/₈-inch-thick slices

¹/₄ to ¹/₃ cup sugar

1¹/₃ pounds bulk country sausage, formed into 8 patties, each 2¹/₂ inches in diameter and ¹/₂ inch thick

To make the biscuits, preheat the oven to 450°F. Sift together the flour, baking powder, and salt into a bowl. Using a pastry blender, cut in the shortening until the mixture is the consistency of coarse meal. Make a well in the center and pour the milk into it. Using a fork, stir and toss the wet and dry ingredients until the mixture holds together. Turn out onto a floured work surface and knead lightly 3 or 4 times, then let stand for 5 minutes.

Roll or pat out the dough ¹/₂ inch thick. Using a biscuit cutter about 2¹/₂ inches in diameter, cut out the biscuits. You should have about 16 biscuits. Arrange them, evenly spaced, on an ungreased baking sheet. Bake for 12 to 15 minutes, or until golden.

(continued)

While the biscuits are baking, fry the apples and sausage: In a large frying pan, melt the butter over medium-high heat. When it begins to bubble, add the apples and stir for about 5 minutes, or until the apples begin to brown. Add the sugar to taste (the amount depends upon the desired sweetness) and continue to cook, stirring often, for about 20 minutes, or until the sugar is melted and beginning to caramelize and the apples are tender.

In a large, nonstick frying pan, fry the sausage patties over medium heat, turning once, for about 5 minutes on each side, or until cooked through and golden brown.

When the biscuits are ready, pile them into a napkin-lined basket and wrap to keep hot. Serve the sausage patties and apples on a warmed platter or on individual plates. Pass the biscuits at the table.

SERVES 4

Alsatian Potatoes and Bacon

Cooks in Alsace are known for their superb sauerkraut, fresh and cured pork, velvety smooth goose foie gras, and equally smooth beer and eaux-de-vie. On November 11, the feast day of Saint Martin, these same cooks traditionally stuff a goose with whole apples and roast it. Months of cold and damp days soon follow. In the past, the Alsatian pantry held little variety during the steel-gray winter. Potatoes, dried apples and other fruits, and bacon were usually on hand, however, and often were combined in a supper-table dish known as *schnitzen*. Choose a good smoky bacon for the best result.

³/₄ pound dried apples

³/₄ pound thick-cut lean slab bacon

6 tablespoons sugar

2¹/₂ tablespoons water

1 cup chicken stock, or more as needed, heated

1¹/₂ to 2 pounds Yukon Gold or other yellow-fleshed potatoes, peeled and cut lengthwise into sixths

2 to 3 teaspoons minced fresh sage, or ³/₄ to 1 teaspoon dried sage

Salt

Freshly ground pepper

1 smoked pork sausage, about ¹/₂ pound, thickly sliced (optional)

Sage or flat-leaf parsley sprigs for garnish

In a bowl, combine the dried apples with water to cover generously and let soak overnight until plumped. Drain well and press out the excess water.

Cut the bacon slices in half crosswise and arrange them on the bottom of a Dutch oven or heavy saucepan.

TRANSPARENT

In a wide saucepan, combine the sugar and the water over medium heat until the sugar dissolves, then bring to a boil and boil for about 5 minutes, or until golden brown and fragrant. Remove from the heat, add the drained apples, and stir to coat well. This step can be difficult, as the caramel will set quickly. Arrange the apples in an even layer on top of the bacon. Pour the chicken stock into the pan that held the apples, place over medium heat, and heat to dissolve any caramelized sugar stuck to the bottom and sides. Pour the stock over the apples and bacon.

Cover, place over medium heat, and bring to a boil. Decrease the heat to low and simmer gently for about 30 minutes, or until the apples are almost tender.

Uncover the pan and scatter the potato pieces evenly over the top, sprinkling them with sage and seasoning generously with salt and pepper. Scatter the sliced sausage over the top. Re-cover and continue to cook, adding more stock if the mixture begins to dry out, for about 20 minutes longer, or until the potatoes are tender. The mixture should be moist when it is done.

Spoon the potatoes and apples into a warmed serving bowl, mixing them together. Arrange the bacon pieces and the sausage on top and garnish with the sage sprigs. Serve at once.

SERVES 6

Although apples are found throughout the world, the ones we eat first emerged ten thousand years ago on the slopes of the Heavenly Mountains in modern Kazakhstan, the historic capital of which is Almaty, roughly "Father of Apples."

Apple and Country Ham Risotto

The first time Browning told Silva about his apple risotto recipe, Silva's Italian eyebrow arched higher than the north tower of the Golden Gate Bridge. Silva, whose Italian grandmother grew up within shouting distance of Milan, home to the only risottos deserving of the name, was not about to accept some crypto-yuppie concoction that would blaspheme the pride of her patrimony. Browning, never one to dodge a culinary combat, took her on, although he has come to acknowledge that pancetta or prosciutto provides an admirable substitute for his beloved cured Kentucky country ham.

5 cups chicken stock

4 tablespoons unsalted butter

3/4 cup diced unpeeled Stayman Winesap, McIntosh, or other firm, sweet-tart apple (1/8-inch dice)

6 tablespoons finely diced country ham (scant 1/4-inch dice)

1 1/2 cups arborio rice

3/4 cup semidry hard cider

Wedge of Asiago cheese

Freshly ground pepper

A few paper-thin apple slices sautéed in unsalted butter for garnish

A few fresh sage leaves for garnish

Pour the stock into a saucepan, place over medium heat, bring to a simmer, and then reduce the heat to very low to keep the liquid hot.

In a frying pan, melt 2 tablespoons of the butter over medium-high heat. Add the apple cubes and sauté, stirring, until lightly browned, about 10 minutes. Do not allow them to soften as they will cook further in the risotto. Remove from the heat and keep warm.

Melt the remaining 2 tablespoons butter in a large saucepan over medium-low heat. Add the ham and rice and stir for 2 to 3 minutes, or until the rice is well coated with the butter. Add the cider and stir for about 2 minutes, or until it is absorbed. Add about 1/2 cup of the hot stock, stir well, and simmer, stirring often, until the stock is absorbed. Continue adding stock, 1/2 cup at a time, and allowing it to be fully absorbed before adding more, until the rice is almost cooked. Add the sautéed apple cubes with the final addition of stock. The rice is ready when it is firm but tender and creamy and the center of each grain is no longer chalky, about 25 minutes' total cooking time. You may not need all of the stock, or you may need more liquid, in which case hot water can be used. Remove from the heat, cover, and let stand for 5 minutes.

Uncover the risotto and spoon onto a warmed serving platter. Using a vegetable peeler, shave curls of Asiago over the top. Follow with a twist of the pepper mill, the sautéed apple slices, and a scattering of sage leaves.

SERVES 4

Roman Pork and Apple Stew

All over northern and eastern Europe, home cooks combine apples and pork into savory stews, probably because pigs have always been the most common farmyard meat and apples the most durable and readily available fruit. The earliest recorded pork and apple stew comes to us from Marcus Gavius Apicius's *Ars magirica*, a Roman work published around the time of Caesar Augustus. *Minutal matianum*, he called it, Matian being a sweet, aromatic apple prized by the Romans. But the key to this rich, spicy dish is garum, the passion of high Roman cuisine, a pint of which in today's currency would cost as much as seven hundred dollars.

And what was this jewel of the spice closet? Fermented fish guts. Specialists would disembowel anchovies or mackerel, then place the entrails with a little sea salt and special herbs into a stone jar, set it in a cool cellar, and wait until the concoction had decomposed. Once the decomposition was complete, the thick liquid would be strained and allowed to ferment until ready.

Diluted with water, garum was given to Roman soldiers as a daily tonic. In the kitchen it was mixed with wine, oil, or vinegar and stored in carefully marked amphorae—or it was added directly to the cook pot. As strange as garum might seem to the modern palate, a version of the same thing, called fish sauce, is commonly used in Southeast Asian cuisine. For our recipe, we combine anchovy paste with Thai fish sauce or, if anchovy paste is unavailable, simply mash tinned anchovies into a paste and add the fish sauce. Don't be afraid. The result is magnificent.

1 bone-in pork shoulder, 6 to 7 pounds

2 tablespoons olive oil

2 leeks, including 2 inches of the pale green, chopped

3 tablespoons chopped fresh cilantro

1 cinnamon stick, 3 inches long

3 tablespoons anchovy paste

4 tablespoons Thai fish sauce (nam pla)

3 to 4 cups chicken stock

1 carrot, peeled and finely diced

3 tablespoons chopped fresh mint, plus extra for garnish

3/4 teaspoon freshly ground pepper

3/4 teaspoon ground cumin

3/4 teaspoon ground coriander

1/3 cup red wine vinegar or cider vinegar

1 tablespoon honey

2 tablespoons brandy or Calvados

2 medium to large Granny Smith, Newtown Pippin, or other tart green apples, unpeeled, cored, and chopped

1 medium to large Fuji, Jonagold, Jonathan, or other sweet or sweet-tart apple, unpeeled, cored, and chopped

3 tablespoons all-purpose flour

3 tablespoons unsalted butter

Bone the pork; you should have about 4 pounds of meat. Cut the meat into 1- to 1¹/₂-inch cubes.

In a Dutch oven or other large, heavy pot, warm the olive oil over medium-high heat. Working in batches, add the pork cubes and brown well on all sides, 5 to 10 minutes. (You may need to drain off some of the released liquid as the pork cooks.) Transfer the pork to a plate.

Add the leeks and cilantro to the oil remaining in the pot and sauté for about 5 minutes, or until softened. Return the pork to the pot and add the cinnamon stick. Stir 2 tablespoons each of the anchovy paste and fish sauce into the chicken stock until well combined. Add just enough stock to the pot to cover the meat. Bring to a simmer over medium heat, decrease the heat to low, and cook, uncovered, for about 45 minutes, or until almost tender. (The stew may be prepared up to this point several hours in advance and refrigerated.)

Meanwhile, in a food processor or a mortar, combine the carrot, mint, pepper, cumin, and coriander and grind to a paste. Transfer to a small saucepan and add the vinegar, honey, brandy, the remaining 1 tablespoon anchovy paste and 2 tablespoons fish sauce, and ¹/₂ cup of the cooking liquid. Stir well and bring to a boil over high heat. Decrease the heat to medium and simmer for 5 minutes to blend the flavors. Remove from the heat.

Stir the apples into the pork mixture, then gradually add the sauce to taste, mixing well. Continue simmering, uncovered, over low heat for another 30 minutes, or until the apples and pork are tender.

About 5 minutes before the pork and apples are done, make a beurre manié by working the flour and butter together to form a paste. Gradually add the beurre manié to the cooking liquid, using only as much as is needed to thicken the liquid to a nice consistency.

Transfer to a warm serving bowl and garnish with chopped mint. Serve immediately.

SERVES 8

Pork and Apple Pie with Horseradish Sauce

The first frozen meat potpies came on the U.S. market in 1951, thanks to C.A. Swanson & Sons. Just two years later, the company introduced the now-legendary turkey TV dinner, a well-balanced meal neatly turned out in a three-section aluminum tray. The idea behind both products was to free the new class of working mothers from the stove, giving them more time to bond with their boomer children and maybe even put up their feet at the end of the day.

But such conveniences never entered farmhouse kitchens, at least not ours. Indeed, our mothers would have laughed at the paucity of protein in those first commercial pies. Of course, some social pundits couldn't wait to weigh in on the new frozen meals too, declaring their introduction the death knell for the American nuclear family, its cohesion certain to be ripped apart by each member opting for a "different flavor."

We offer this apple-loaded, family-friendly pie, which carves into four nice nuclear portions, in tribute to those days before the frozen-food aisle became the most popular thoroughfare in neighborhood markets.

PASTRY

2 cups all-purpose flour

1 teaspoon salt

1 teaspoon dried fines herbes (chives, parsley, tarragon, and chervil)

²/₃ cup chilled solid vegetable shortening

4 to 6 tablespoons ice water

PORK AND APPLE FILLING

4 Granny Smith, Newtown Pippin, or other tart apples, peeled, halved, cored, and sliced

1 pound lean ground pork

3 tablespoons minced yellow onion

1 tablespoon brown sugar

2 teaspoons minced fresh thyme

1¹/₂ teaspoons minced fresh sage

1 teaspoon salt

• • • • •

1 small egg lightly beaten with ³/₄ teaspoon milk

HORSERADISH SAUCE

1 cup sour cream

¹/₄ cup prepared horseradish

To make the pastry, stir together the flour, salt, and fines herbes in a bowl. Add half of the shortening and cut in with a pastry blender until the mixture is the consistency of coarse meal. Then add the remaining shortening and cut in until pea-sized particles form. Add the ice water, 1 tablespoon at a time, tossing and turning the mixture lightly with a fork to moisten the dough evenly. Use only as much water as is necessary for the dough to come together. Gently gather the dough into a ball, divide in half, and flatten each half into a thick disk. Wrap separately in plastic wrap and chill for at least 1 hour.

Preheat the oven to 400°F.

To make the filling, place the apples in a large bowl. Scatter the pork over the top, then mix with a large spoon to distribute it evenly. Sprinkle the onion, sugar, thyme, sage, and salt over the top and mix again until thoroughly combined.

Place 1 dough disk on a lightly floured work surface and roll out into an 11-inch round about 1/8 inch thick. Drape the round around the rolling pin and transfer to a 9-inch pie pan, gently easing it into the bottom and sides. Trim the overhang so that it extends about 1 inch beyond the rim of the pie pan, then fold the edges under. Roll out the remaining disk in the same manner for use as the top crust.

Spoon the apple-pork filling into the pie shell, mounding it slightly in the center. Drape the second pastry round around the rolling pin and let it fall gently over the filling. Trim the overhang so it extends about 1/2 inch beyond the rim of the pan, fold the edge under, and flute attractively. Cut a few small vents in the top, then brush the surface evenly with the egg-milk mixture.

Bake for about 1 hour, or until the pastry is shiny and golden and the apples, when pierced through a vent, are tender. Transfer to a wire rack to cool.

Meanwhile, make the sauce: In a small bowl, whisk together the sour cream and horseradish.

Serve the pie warm or at room temperature. Pass the sauce at the table.

SERVES 4

Italian Sausage–Stuffed Apples

Apples marry successfully with countless disparate foods, from the lofty to the every-day. On the high end of that scale rests New York–based, Hungarian-born restaurant consultant George Lang's foie gras proposal, as reported in a January 1999 issue of the *New Yorker*: "Let's try a . . . sand-wich in which the top and the bottom of an apple [are] baked and the filling . . . is goose liver." A rather ritzy—and pricy—lunchbox stuffer, unless, of course, you are fattening the birds yourself.

Not long after that article, Browning actually tried to sell Silva on the idea of a foie gras–stuffed baked apple, a dish he read about in a *New York Times* restaurant review. But Silva stood firm: "If I get my hands on a foie gras, an apple is the last place I plan to stow it. It's kind of a sow's ear, silk purse question."

"But we need stuffed apple recipes in this book," Browning insisted. "People expect them. Turn down my foie gras idea, and you have to come up with your own."

"You know that my mother's parents came from northern Italy, apple country, and even though my mother didn't stuff our orchard harvest, one of her fennel-sausage stuffings would be quite tasty lodged inside a baking apple," Silva shot back. "Let's wait until our royalties pour in before we start buying foie gras for testing apple recipes."

And thus this pennywise recipe was born.

6 ounces coarse country bread, crusts removed

$2/3$ cup milk

8 Rome Beauty, Stayman Winesap, Jonathan, Jonagold, or other good baking apples

Juice of 1 lemon

10 ounces Italian sweet fennel sausage, casings removed

3 to 4 ounces imported provolone cheese, finely diced

1 egg, lightly beaten

$2^{1}/_{2}$ tablespoons finely chopped fresh flat-leaf parsley

Salt

Freshly ground pepper

Preheat the oven to 350°F.

Pull apart the bread into large pieces and place in a bowl. Pour in the milk and let stand while you prepare the apples.

Cut a 1/2-inch slice off the stem end of each apple and discard the tops. With a melon baller or grapefruit spoon, scoop out the core from each apple, being careful not to pierce the blossom end, and discard. Then continue to scoop out the apple flesh to form a hollow cavity with sturdy sides. Discard the pulp or reserve for another use. Rub the apple cavities with the lemon juice and set aside.

Squeeze the bread to press out as much milk as possible. Place the bread in a bowl and add the sausage, cheese, egg, and parsley. Mix well, then season with salt and pepper and mix again.

Spoon the sausage mixture into the apple cavities, dividing it evenly and mounding the tops. Place the apples in a baking dish large enough to hold them in a single layer. Pour water into the dish to a depth of about 1/4 inch.

Bake for about 45 minutes, or until the apples are tender when pierced with a sharp knife. Serve hot directly from the dish.

SERVES 8

A traditional Sicilian girl would toss an apple into the street and watch to see who picked it up. If it was a boy, fable had it that they would marry within the year. If it was a woman, she would have to wait a year. And if it was a priest, she would die a virgin.

Jonathan

Iranian Veal-Stuffed Apples

Long before our European ancestors knew that there was more to a good meal than quarreling over flame-licked bear bones just beyond the cave door, the Persians were sitting down to sumptuous feasts built around fruits and vegetables plucked from their own elaborate household gardens. Indeed, the culinary genius of the sophisticated Farsi-speaking cook fueled the rise of respectable kitchens from the eastern Mediterranean to the jungles of Sumatra. No doubt a version of this classic dish was on Esfahān tables not long after the earliest Persian apple trees yielded their first harvest.

10 small to medium Rome Beauty, Jonagold, Stayman Winesap, or other good baking apples

1½ teaspoons granulated sugar

3 tablespoons clarified butter

2 small yellow onions, finely chopped

1 pound ground veal

1⅓ cups water

2½ tablespoons long-grain white rice

¾ teaspoon ground cinnamon

Salt

Freshly ground pepper

3 tablespoons cider vinegar, or more if needed

3 tablespoons packed brown sugar, or more if needed

Cut a ½-inch slice off the stem end of each apple, reserving the tops. With a melon baller or grapefruit spoon, scoop out the core from each apple, being careful not to pierce the blossom end, and discard. Continue to scoop out the apple flesh to form a hollow cavity with sturdy sides. Set the removed pulp aside. Sprinkle the apple cavities with the granulated sugar and set aside with the tops.

Preheat the oven to 350°F.

In a frying pan, warm the clarified butter over medium-high heat. Add the onions and cook, stirring, for about 5 minutes, or until translucent. Add the veal and cook, breaking up the meat with the spoon, for 3 to 5 minutes, or until it is no longer pink. Add ⅓ cup of the water, the rice, and the cinnamon and stir well. Season with salt and pepper and remove from the heat.

Spoon the veal mixture into the apple cavities, dividing it evenly. Replace the tops. Pour the remaining 1 cup water into a baking dish large enough to hold the apples in a single layer. Arrange the stuffed apples in the dish, and then surround them with about three-fourths of the reserved apple pulp (reserve the remaining pulp for another use). Cover the dish with a lid or with aluminum foil.

Bake for about 30 minutes, then uncover the dish. Stir together the vinegar and brown sugar, mix into the pulp and juices in the bottom of the baking dish, and then baste the apples with the mixture. Continue to bake, uncovered, for 15 to 25 minutes longer, or until the apples are tender when pierced with a sharp knife.

Transfer the apples to a warmed serving platter and keep warm. Pass the pulp and liquid in the bottom of the baking dish through a sieve placed over a small saucepan.

(continued)

(Iranian Veal-Stuffed Apples, continued)

Place over medium heat and simmer until reduced to a nice sauce consistency. Taste and adjust with more cider vinegar and/or brown sugar to achieve a good sweet-sour balance.

Spoon the sauce over the apples and serve at once.

SERVES 8 TO 10

VARIATION: An equal amount of dried yellow split peas can be used in place of the rice.

Calf's Liver with Applejack

Now and then all you want is simple. This quick dish, common in every family kitchen and country bistro in Brittany and Normandy, albeit made with Calvados in those climes, couldn't be quicker. Indeed, quickness is the key. Three minutes, or three and a half for a thick piece of liver, is the absolute maximum for a warm, sweet, creamy texture. (If you insist on having your liver well done, don't waste the applejack. Cover the organ with fried onions and try not to think of shoe leather or dorm food.)

2 tablespoons unsalted butter

4 slices calf's liver, 5 to 6 ounces each

Salt

2 to 3 tablespoons applejack

Freshly ground pepper

In a large frying pan, melt the butter over medium-high heat. Add the liver pieces, season with salt, and cook for about 1$\frac{1}{2}$ minutes, or until nicely seared on the first side. Turn the liver over, cook for 30 seconds, then sprinkle with the applejack. Continue to cook for about 1 minute for medium-rare—the best way to eat calf's liver.

Transfer to a warmed platter, grind pepper over the top, and serve immediately.

SERVES 4

Sauerkraut-Stuffed Apples

Nineteenth-century American cookbooks nearly all contained some sort of apple and sauerkraut recipe. Unless your family came from Germany, Poland, or the old Czechoslovakia, your mother probably never opened the cookbook to that page. Too bad. This version, updated with the addition of mushrooms—we use portobello, but any earthy-flavored variety will do—makes a refreshingly spicy dish, and despite the slight amount of lean bacon, it will even please your HMO.

1¹/₂ cups fresh sauerkraut, rinsed and well drained

2 slices thick-cut lean slab bacon, diced

³/₄ cup chopped fresh portobello mushroom

Seeds from 4 to 6 cardamom pods, crushed

¹/₄ teaspoon caraway seeds

Freshly ground pepper

4 Jonagold, Stayman Winesap, Jonathan, or other good baking apples

¹/₂ to 1 cup fresh cider

Preheat the oven to 350°F.

In a bowl, combine the sauerkraut, bacon, mushroom, cardamom, caraway seeds, and pepper to taste. Mix well.

Cut a ¹/₂-inch slice off the stem end of each apple and discard the tops. With a melon baller or grapefruit spoon, scoop out the core from each apple, being careful not to pierce the blossom end, and discard. Then continue to scoop out the apple flesh to form a hollow cavity with sturdy sides. Reserve the removed pulp.

Spoon the sauerkraut mixture into the apple cavities, dividing it evenly and mounding the tops. Place the apples in a baking dish large enough to hold them in a single layer. Pour the cider into the dish to a depth of about ¹/₄ inch. Distribute the reserved pulp evenly around the apples.

Bake for 35 to 45 minutes, or until the apples are tender when pierced with a sharp knife. Serve hot directly from the dish, spooning the dish juices around the apples.

SERVES 4

Iranian Lamb and Apple Sauce with Chelou

Nearly every Iranian is brought up to be a rice expert. Men and women alike are expected to be able to discuss the relative merits of an unaged basmati rice versus one that has sat for a year or even two years. Likewise, the best Iranian cooks can deliver up a respectable number of both main types of rice dish: *chelou*, plain rice that is traditionally served with a sauce, or *khoresh*; and *polo*, which calls for mixing various ingredients into the rice, much like a pilaf. A *khoresh* that is spooned over a buttery mound of *chelou* usually relies on the seasonal cupboard, combining lamb or beef with fresh (apples, cherries, quinces) or dried (apricots, peaches, prunes) fruits and/or vegetables. Here, a good cooking apple holds its own in a perfume of Near Eastern spices.

LAMB AND APPLE SAUCE

3½ tablespoons clarified unsalted butter or vegetable oil

2 yellow onions, finely chopped

¾ teaspoon ground turmeric

⅛ teaspoon ground cinnamon

Pinch ground cardamom

2 pounds boneless lamb shoulder or other lamb stew meat, trimmed of visible fat and cut into ¾-inch cubes

1½ cups hot water

Salt

Freshly ground pepper

4 Jonathan, Granny Smith, Pink Lady, or other semitart or tart apples, peeled, quartered, cored, and sliced lengthwise

About 2 teaspoons freshly squeezed lime juice

About 2 teaspoons brown sugar

CHELOU

2 tablespoons salt

2 cups basmati rice

5 tablespoons unsalted butter

5 tablespoons water

• • • • •

Cilantro sprigs for garnish

GRANNY SMITH

To make the sauce, warm 1¹/₂ tablespoons of the clarified butter in a deep frying pan over medium-high heat. Add the onions and cook, stirring, for about 1 minute. Sprinkle with the turmeric, cinnamon, and cardamom and continue to cook, stirring, for about 4 minutes, or until the onions are translucent. Add the lamb and cook, stirring often, until the meat is lightly browned, about 3 minutes. Add the hot water, season with salt and a generous measure of pepper, and bring to a simmer. Cover, decrease the heat to medium, and simmer gently for 45 to 60 minutes, or until the lamb is nearly tender.

While the lamb is cooking, make the *chelou*: Fill a large, heavy saucepan three-fourths full of water and bring to a rolling boil. Add the salt and rice and return to a boil, stirring occasionally. Boil, uncovered, for 8 to 10 minutes, or until the rice is barely cooked. Drain in a colander and rinse with hot water.

In a small saucepan, melt the butter with the water until the mixture begins to bubble. Pour half of the butter mixture into a heavy-bottomed saucepan or deep, flameproof baking dish with a tight-fitting lid and tip and tilt the pan to coat the bottom and sides. Spoon about half of the rice into the pan, forming an even layer. Mound the remaining rice in the center. With the handle of a wooden spoon, drive a deep hole into the center of the mound, then drizzle the remaining butter mixture evenly over the mound. Cover the pan or dish with a tight-fitting lid and place over medium-low heat for 10 minutes. Decrease the heat to low and continue to cook for about 30 minutes longer, or until the rice is fluffy, light, and tender.

Just before the meat is ready, warm the remaining 2 tablespoons clarified butter in a large frying pan over medium-high heat. Add the apple slices and cook, turning as necessary, for about 5 minutes, or until they begin to take on color but are still firm. Remove from the heat.

Add the apple slices to the lamb and cook, uncovered, stirring gently, for 5 to 10 minutes, or until the apples are just tender and are infused with the spices. Do not overcook, or the slices will break up. Stir in the lime juice and brown sugar, adjusting the amounts as needed to achieve a pleasant sweet-sour balance.

Stir and toss the rice with a fork to distribute the butter evenly, then spoon onto a warmed serving platter. Spoon the meat sauce into a warmed serving bowl and garnish with cilantro sprigs. Serve at once with the rice.

SERVES 6

SIDE DISHES

Appalachian Cider-Baked Beans

If beans aren't the world's most ubiquitous vegetable, they should be. From Shanghai to Pippa Passes, Kentucky (deep in the mountains), beans have been a staple of survival for centuries (millennia in China). Alas, too many of us who slogged through school lunch programs in the postwar era remember watery "soup beans" with a shudder of nausea. And what a pity! For up the hollow or over the next ridge, mountain mothers were making magnificent pots of stewed and baked beans. This version, adapted from my own childhood with a touch of French Canadian influence (the whole hidden onions at the center), is hardy enough to make a meal in itself. The cider sweetens the beans and adds bloom to their own natural fragrance. —FB

3 cups dried pinto beans

1 bottle (750 ml) semisweet hard cider, or 3 cups fresh cider

$1/2$ pound salt pork, thinly sliced

2 small yellow onions

6 tablespoons sorghum, or $1/2$ cup molasses

1 tablespoon dry mustard

2 teaspoons salt

Pick over the beans and discard any stones or misshapen beans. Rinse well and place in a large bowl. Add cold water to cover by 3 inches, cover, and let soak for 12 hours.

Drain the beans and transfer to a heavy saucepan. Add the cider and bring slowly to a boil over medium heat. Boil gently, uncovered, for about 30 minutes. Remove from the heat and drain the beans, reserving the cider.

Meanwhile, preheat the oven to 300°F.

Layer half of the salt pork slices on the bottom of a 2-quart ceramic bean pot or other deep baking dish. Spoon the beans into the bean pot, then bury the onions in the beans. In a small saucepan, combine the sorghum, mustard, and salt and place over medium heat to dissolve the mustard and salt. Pour the hot mixture evenly over the beans, and top with the remaining salt pork slices. Pour in the reserved cider and add hot water as needed to cover the beans. Cover the bean pot.

Bake for about 4 hours, then uncover the pot and add more water if the beans seem too dry. Re-cover and continue to bake until the beans are tender, 1 to 2 hours longer. The timing will depend upon the age of the beans. Serve hot directly from the pot.

SERVES 8

Fujis and Flowering Kale

The pairing of apples with various offspring of the cabbage family is a popular one throughout central and eastern Europe and into Scandinavia, the seasoning shifting with the national borders. Here, a pretty head of ivory-edged red flowering kale, sometimes called ornamental kale or salad savoy and commonly spotted dressing up flower beds outside corporate offices, joins a couple of equally comely sweet apples in a dish that rides nicely alongside a pork roast or a lamb stew.

2 tablespoons safflower oil

2 Fuji or Pink Lady apples, unpeeled, quartered, cored, and sliced

$1/2$ teaspoon fennel seeds, crushed

1 head red flowering kale, about 9 inches in diameter, cored and leaves separated

Salt

2 to 4 tablespoons balsamic or cider vinegar

In a large frying pan, warm the safflower oil over medium heat. Add the apples and sauté, turning as needed, until they begin to take on color, about 7 minutes, adding the fennel seeds during the last 2 minutes.

Add the kale leaves, cover, and cook for about 10 minutes, or until wilted and tender. Check occasionally, and if the leaves begin to scorch, add a little water. If at the end of cooking there is excess water, uncover and raise the heat to high to cook off the moisture.

Season with salt, then stir in the vinegar to taste. Transfer to a warmed serving dish and serve at once.

SERVES 4 TO 6

VARIATION: Substitute 1 small head red cabbage, cored and leaves separated, for the kale.

The Swedenborgian mystic John Chapman, better known as Johnny Appleseed, developed more apple varieties in his wild-seedling nurseries than any other American in history.

Judy Stone's Apple Chutney

While writing this book, we hosted a couple of so-called apple cook-offs, to which we invited lots of opinionated food-loving friends to taste up to a dozen different recipes in a single evening. Most folks showed up with a bottle of cider, or sometimes wine or champagne. On Christmas Eve, we received a box of exquisite chocolates from one couple and a jar of preserved Meyer lemons from another. But our friend Judy Stone, a well-known writer on international cinema and a damned good cook, came bearing the same wonderful house gift for both events, her now-legendary apple chutney. Each time we put it out on the table with our various apple concoctions, and each time it ended up being one of the most popular dishes of the night. She kindly parted with her secret recipe.

4 or 5 Granny Smith, Newtown Pippin, or other tart apples, peeled, cored, and coarsely chopped

$1/2$ cup dried pears, coarsely chopped

$1/2$ cup dried peaches, coarsely chopped

$1/2$ cup dried apricots, coarsely chopped

$1/3$ cup golden raisins

5 to 7 cloves garlic, mashed

2-inch piece fresh ginger, peeled and grated

$2^1/2$ cups sugar, or more to taste

$1^1/4$ cups red wine vinegar, or more to taste

2 teaspoons salt

$1/2$ to 1 teaspoon cayenne pepper, or more to taste

In a heavy enameled or other nonreactive pot, combine the apples, pears, peaches, apricots, raisins, garlic, ginger, sugar, vinegar, salt, and cayenne pepper. Bring to a boil over high heat, reduce the heat to medium, and simmer, stirring often and adjusting the heat as needed to prevent scorching, for 30 to 40 minutes, or until the mixture is the texture of old-fashioned fruit preserves. Taste and adjust with more sugar, vinegar, or cayenne if necessary.

Remove from the heat and let cool to room temperature. The mixture will continue to thicken. Spoon into clean jars, cover tightly, and refrigerate for about 2 weeks before serving to allow the flavors to mellow. The chutney will keep for up to 2 months in the refrigerator.

MAKES ABOUT $3^1/2$ CUPS

Burning Love

....

When Elisabeth Dyssegaard told us that one of the favored dishes of grim Calvinist Denmark was called burning love, or *braendende kaerlighed*, we couldn't resist. On those long, dark, windswept winter evenings, who wouldn't want to slip a bit of burning ardor into a lover's mouth (even if it wasn't on the menu for *Babette's Feast*).

SAUCE

3 slices thick-cut lean slab bacon, finely diced

2 Jonathan, Stayman Winesap, Russet, or other aromatic saucing apples, unpeeled, cored, and finely diced

1 large yellow onion, finely diced

Salt

Freshly ground pepper

MASHED POTATOES

2 pounds potatoes, peeled and cut into 3-inch pieces (see note)

3 to 4 tablespoons unsalted butter, cut into small pieces

About ⅔ cup half-and-half, heated

Salt

Freshly ground pepper

To make the sauce, cook the bacon in a heavy frying pan over medium heat for a few minutes, or until the fat begins to render. Add the apples and onion and cook, stirring occasionally, for 12 to 15 minutes, or until the mixture has a nice sauce consistency but the apples have not completely broken down. Season with salt and pepper. Keep warm.

While the sauce is cooking, make the potatoes: Bring a saucepan filled with salted water to a boil. Add the potatoes and cook for 15 to 20 minutes, or until tender. Drain well and return the potatoes to the pan over high heat, turning them to prevent scorching and sticking, for about 1 minute, or until any moisture evaporates. Pass the potatoes through a ricer or food mill held over a warmed bowl, or place them in the bowl and mash with a potato masher. Scatter the butter over the potatoes and then gradually add the half-and-half, stirring vigorously with a spoon until smooth and creamy but not too loose. Season with salt and pepper.

Reheat the sauce, if necessary, and spoon into a serving dish. Serve the potatoes immediately and pass the sauce at the table.

SERVES 4

NOTE: Baking potatoes produce fluffy mashed potatoes, while yellow-fleshed or white- or red-skinned potatoes result in a denser, creamier finish. Opt for what you favor.

Fox Mountain Parsnips

{pictured as a side dish to Pork Loin Stuffed with Fresh and Dried Apples on page 77}

In winter I want roots. Turnips, salsify, carrots, celeriac, exotic potatoes (tubers really). It wasn't always so. Like most children I regarded a plate of parsnips or turnips as palate punishment. At some point in high school, my taste buds matriculated, probably with the old southern standard scalloped parsnips with bacon: sliced parsnips sprinkled with a little flour, stacked in a baking dish, topped with bacon slices, moistened with some water, covered, and baked until tender. Mother was a good cook, but this dish is better (and healthier). It bubbled up out of the vegetable drawer one winter afternoon in Kentucky some years ago, and it has won applause from culinary grinches on both coasts. The cider enriches the earthiness of the parsnips, and the dried apples add snap. We named it in honor of Fox Mountain, just out the ridge from the orchard. —FB

1 slice thick-cut lean slab bacon

12 dried apple slices

About 2 cups dry hard cider

3 parsnips, each about 8 inches long and 1¹/₂ inches in diameter at the stem end, peeled, halved crosswise, and sliced lengthwise ¹/₄ inch thick

¹/₃ cup heavy cream

Salt

Freshly ground pepper

In a frying pan, fry the bacon over medium heat for 3 to 5 minutes, or until the fat is rendered. Add the apple slices and 1 cup of the cider and simmer, uncovered, for 20 minutes, or until the apples begin to soften.

Add the parsnips and enough of the remaining cider just to cover them, and continue to simmer for about 15 minutes, or until the parsnips are nearly tender. Add the cream and simmer for 5 minutes longer, or until the parsnips are tender and the cooking liquid is reduced to a creamy consistency. Remove the bacon and discard.

Season with salt and pepper and transfer to a warmed serving dish. Serve at once.

SERVES 4

Purée of Apple and Celeriac

The homely celeriac, a swollen, knobby, rough-skinned root, is often whipped with potatoes and cream for a simple midwinter purée. Savvy cooks know that apples and celeriac are seasonal soul mates, too, and the perfect partners in this cool-weather union.

3 McIntosh, Jonathan, Empire, or other aromatic saucing apples, or a mixture, peeled, cored, and diced

2 small or 1 large celeriac (celery root), peeled and diced

$1/2$ to $2/3$ cup heavy cream, heated

$1/2$ teaspoon ground ginger

Salt

Freshly ground white pepper

Minced fresh flat-leaf parsley for garnish

Measure the diced apples and celeriac; you should have about 3 cups of each. (If you have too much celeriac, toss it with a little lemon juice and save for adding to the soup pot or a salad the next day.)

In a saucepan, combine the celeriac with water to cover by 3 or 4 inches, bring to a boil over high heat, and boil for 10 to 12 minutes, or until half-cooked. Add the apples and continue to cook for 10 to 15 minutes, or until the celeriac and the apples are very tender.

Drain well. Working in batches if necessary, transfer to a food processor or blender. With the motor running, gradually pour in enough cream to create a thick, smooth purée. Season with the ginger, salt, and white pepper.

Transfer to a warmed bowl, sprinkle with the parsley, and serve immediately.

SERVES 6

"No fruit is more to our English taste than the Apple. Let the Frenchman have his Pear, the Italian his Fig, the Jamaican may retain his farinaceous banana and the Malay his Durian, but for us the Apple."

—Edward Bunyard,
 The Anatomy of Dessert, 1929

Real Applesauce

I was girding myself for Browning's reaction as I dialed the phone. "Hi," I said, pausing only a moment and then blurting out my request. "You know, we need an applesauce recipe."

"But everybody knows how to make applesauce," he snapped back, his voice a bellow of exasperation. "It's the next lesson after boiling eggs."

"Believe me," I said, "lots of people don't know. They think their grandmothers are going to make it for them, or that you just buy a jar of it at the supermarket. Please, we need a basic applesauce recipe. Does it help that this time I agree with you, that we don't need to peel the apples?"

"But that's all it is, apples, and maybe some sugar if they aren't good apples. If you want to get fancy, you add a little ground spice. But a recipe? That's crazy."

"Trust me on this one, Browning. An apple book needs an applesauce recipe."

"Okay, okay, you win this time," he barked back, notes of both defeat and sarcasm in his voice. "So here's my recipe: 'First, wash off all the road dust. . . .'" —SS

8 good saucing apples, a mixture of sweet and tart such as Lodi, Macoun, Empire, Jonathan, Stayman Winesap, and Cortland

1/2 cup water

Sugar

Ground cinnamon or freshly grated nutmeg (optional)

Cut the apples into fourths or eighths, but do not peel or core them. Drop into a heavy saucepan, add the water, place over medium heat, cover, and cook, uncovering and stirring every now and again, for 15 to 20 minutes, or until the apples are very soft. To test, press with the tines of a fork or a potato masher; the apples should collapse easily.

Remove from the heat and pass through a food mill into a bowl. Taste, and if not sweet enough, add some sugar. Season with the cinnamon or nutmeg. Serve warm, at room temperature, or cold.

SERVES 4

Lynn Meyer's Haroseth

Lynn Meyer couldn't help it. Growing up a precocious child on Manhattan's Upper West Side, surrounded by books and music, taken to theater and museums on a regular basis, she still suffered serious deprivation, and it was worse come Passover. The kitchen was not, shall we say, her mother's most successful passion. The bitter herbs of the seder table were, well, bitter. But the haroseth! "It's supposed to symbolize the mortar the Hebrew slaves were forced to make in ancient Egypt. But it's not supposed to taste like gravel!" By the time she took over her own kitchen and surrounded her own children with the same cultural riches her parents gave her, she determined that good food would also become part of their heritage. Why not lay a seder table that recalled the memory of pain and perseverance but didn't reenact gustatory suffering? As for the haroseth, there seemed no reason why the mixture of apples, honey, and nuts shouldn't be delicious, and this version is.

2 Pink Lady, Arkansas Black, or Suncrisp apples (see note), peeled or unpeeled, halved, cored, and chopped into 1/4-inch dice

1 to 2 teaspoons freshly squeezed lemon juice

1 cup finely chopped walnuts

About 1/4 teaspoon ground cinnamon

Freshly grated nutmeg

About 2 tablespoons honey

1 tablespoon Calvados, or to taste

In a bowl, toss the apples with the lemon juice to coat evenly. Add the walnuts, cinnamon, and several gratings of nutmeg and again toss to distribute evenly. Add enough honey to bind the mixture lightly, then gently stir in the Calvados.

MAKES ABOUT 3 CUPS

NOTE: A mixture of yellow- and red-skinned apples would be nice here, if you decide not to peel them. Also, try to select apples that do not turn brown when cut. Finally, the apples need to be good keepers—that is, they must store well until spring.

DESSERTS & BEVERAGES

Apple Dumplings

As sure as Halloween brought the end of the last crimson maple leaves, and the crisp clear skies of October turned sullen and gray with threatening snow clouds, most of us around the orchard knew that apple dumpling time was not far off. Apple dumplings are an indulgent dessert, a sinful compensation intended to turn our gaze inward and away from the bleakness of impending winter. They must surely have served the same purpose for the stern New Englanders who ate them for Sunday dinner after the stern sermons. We never had to suffer the sermons in our house, but we loved the indulgence just the same—although seldom more than two or three times a winter. —FB

PASTRY

2 cups all-purpose flour

1/2 teaspoon salt

2/3 cup chilled solid vegetable shortening

3 tablespoons chilled unsalted butter

4 to 6 tablespoons ice water

. . . . .

6 Rome Beauty, Braeburn, Stayman Winesap, eastern Golden Delicious, Jonathan, or other good baking apples

6 tablespoons unsalted butter

About 3 tablespoons sugar, plus 1/2 to 3/4 cup for the baking dish

11/2 teaspoons ground cinnamon

Freshly grated nutmeg

Water or fresh cider as needed

To make the pastry, in a bowl, stir together the flour and salt. Add half each of the shortening and butter and cut them in with a pastry blender until the mixture is the consistency of coarse meal. Then add the remaining butter and shortening and cut them in until pea-sized particles form. Add the ice water, 1 tablespoon at a time, tossing and turning the mixture lightly with a fork

to moisten the dough evenly. Use only as much water as is necessary for the dough to come together. Gently gather the dough into a ball, divide in half, and flatten each half into a thick disk. Wrap separately in plastic wrap and chill for about 1 hour.

Preheat the oven to 400°F. Butter a baking dish large enough to hold the wrapped apples upright without crowding.

To make the dumplings, working with 1 apple at a time and starting at the stem end, core the apple to within about 1/2 inch of the blossom end, taking care not to cut through the bottom. Remove a few horizontal strips of peel from around the equator of the apple to prevent it from bursting during baking. When all of the apples are cored, drop 1 tablespoon butter, a heaping teaspoon of sugar, 1/4 teaspoon cinnamon, and a couple of gratings of nutmeg into each hollowed-out core.

On a lightly floured work surface, roll out 1 pastry disk into a rectangle about 1/8 inch thick. Cut out 3 equal squares. Place an apple in the center of each square and bring up the corners, gathering the dough around the apple in pleats, and then pressing the edges of the pleats

(continued)

together to cover the apple completely. Repeat with the remaining pastry disk and apples.

Place the wrapped apples in the prepared baking dish. Pour water or cider into the dish to a depth of 1/4 inch. Sprinkle 1/2 to 3/4 cup sugar around the apples; the amount will depend upon the size of the dish.

Bake until the pastry is set, about 15 minutes. Decrease the temperature to 350°F and continue to bake for about 45 minutes, or until the pastry is golden and a skewer thrust into an apple meets little resistance. Remove from the oven and let cool in the dish for about 30 minutes. A syrup will have formed around the dumplings.

Transfer the dumplings to individual plates and spoon the syrup from the dish over the top. Serve warm.

SERVES 6

VARIATIONS: If desired, omit the sugar in the baking dish and serve the dumplings with Blush Syrup (following) in place of the syrup from the dish or with hard sauce, the traditional topping for apple dumplings: Cream together equal parts unsalted butter and confectioners' sugar and finish with a little vanilla extract or, better yet, Calvados, Cognac, or bourbon. It should be made in advance, chilled, and placed on the top of the dumplings as they are served. A teaspoon per dumpling is all you'll need.

Blush Syrup

"Peel the damned apples this time!" Silva barks at me, and now and then I humbly acknowledge that she's right. There are occasions, like her transporting Italian fritters, when the apples must be peeled. But then what to do with those peelings. Throw them out? Never. Too much flavor and vitamins. So here's what you do: add them to a simple sugar syrup, which you can keep in the fridge for months and use whenever you need to doll up a dessert. It's not only tasty, but as beautiful as liquid roses. —FB

2 cups water

2 cups sugar

Peelings from 3 or 4 red apples

In a heavy saucepan over medium-high heat, combine the water and sugar. Bring to a simmer, stirring constantly to dissolve the sugar. Add the peelings and continue to cook, stirring often, for 10 to 15 minutes, or until thickened to a rosy, medium-thick syrup. Let cool before using.

MAKES ABOUT 3 CUPS

Berkeley Apple-Pecan-Cranberry Crisp

Judith Dunham tends a few organically grown Gravensteins in her backyard in Berkeley, California, but she grew up on the East Coast, where her mother regularly turned the fall crop from a couple of backyard trees into an endless stream of apple pies and apple crisps. Since Gravensteins ripen in the summer, and Judith has strong autumn apple memories, she freezes some of her harvest for when the days turn cold. She joins Browning in the peel-on school—"Frank is a cook after my own lazy heart"—but sides with Silva in eschewing cinnamon in favor of grpimd ginger when it comes to crisps. Indeed, she even admits to gilding the lily occasionally by adding a scattering of crystallized ginger to the whipped cream.

5 cups sliced unpeeled Jonagold, Braeburn, or other good pie apples

1 cup fresh cranberries

1/4 cup plus 3 tablespoons firmly packed brown sugar

1 1/2 teaspoons ground ginger

Juice of 1/2 lemon

3/4 cup unbleached all-purpose flour

1/4 cup old-fashioned baby or regular rolled oats

1/2 cup pecan halves or pieces, lightly toasted and chopped

6 tablespoons unsalted butter, cut into small pieces

Whipped cream or vanilla ice cream as an accompaniment (optional)

Preheat the oven to 375°F.

Place the apple slices and cranberries in a 9-inch pie plate. Add 3 tablespoons of the brown sugar, 1/2 teaspoon of the ground ginger, and the lemon juice, and toss to combine. Pat the fruit to compress it in the dish, and flatten the top evenly.

In a bowl, combine the flour, oats, the remaining 1/4 cup brown sugar, the chopped nuts, and the remaining 1 teaspoon ginger. Cut in the butter with two knives, then use your fingers, working quickly to distribute the butter evenly. Sprinkle the topping evenly over the fruit, then press it down lightly with your fingers.

Bake for 40 to 45 minutes, or until the topping is crisp and golden and the fruit is soft and bubbly. Serve hot, warm, or at room temperature with whipped cream or ice cream.

SERVES 6

Apple and Currant Galettes

One spring evening, while supping at one of those oh-so-trendy Berkeley eateries where plain food is dressed up in inflationary names, we finished off with a lovely, flat little apple pastry that the chef called an apple galette. Other places call the same thing an apple *croustade*. The idea is simple: roll out a nice piece of pie dough or puff pastry, place a fruit and/or nut mixture at the center, and roll up the edges into a stylish ring, leaving only about half the filling exposed at the center. Our version uses dried currants (which are really Zante grapes, dried), but you might use fresh or dried blueberries or even cranberries.

In any case, you should feel just a little bit wilder eating a galette than an apple pie. The word *galette* seems to trace its origin via Old French to the Celtic (or Gaulic) *galet*, meaning a small stone or pebble, which was represented by a bean in the classic *galette des rois*, served on the feast of Twelfth Night. And Twelfth Night, like so many Christian feast days, is only a slightly veiled version of the ancient pagan feast of Saturnalia, where the wanton revelry was led by a lucky fellow chosen in a ritual that involved drawing beans. The Christians took to hiding a fava bean in a piece of sweet cake, and the one who got the bean was named king or queen of Twelfth Night. You can do the same thing by hiding a hazelnut in one of the apple galettes and awarding an extra shot of Calvados to your lucky guest.

1½ tablespoons unsalted butter

2 eastern Golden Delicious, Jonagold, York, Jonathan, or other good pie apples, peeled, cored, and cut lengthwise into eighths

2 tablespoons Calvados

½ teaspoon peeled, grated fresh ginger

¼ cup plus 3 tablespoons semisweet hard cider

About 3 tablespoons dried currants

About 1 pound puff pastry, thawed if frozen

About 2 tablespoons Blush Syrup (page 112)

In a frying pan, melt the butter over medium-high heat. Add the apple pieces and sauté, turning as needed, for about 5 minutes, or until beginning to turn golden. Sprinkle with Calvados and ignite with a match. When the flames die out, add the ginger and 3 tablespoons of the hard cider and bring to a simmer over medium heat. Continue to simmer for 2 to 3 minutes, or until the cider has evaporated. Remove from the heat and set aside to cool.

Meanwhile, preheat the oven to 400°F. In a small saucepan, combine the currants and the remaining ¼ cup cider over medium heat. Bring to a simmer and cook for about 2 minutes, or until plumped. Drain and set aside.

(continued)

On a lightly floured board, roll out the pastry about 1/8 inch thick. Cut out eight 4-inch squares. Place 2 of the cooled apple pieces, rounded sides up, in the center of each square. Bring the sides of each square up and fold inward to create a freeform pastry shell, pinching and tucking the edges as necessary and leaving the apples uncovered. Sprinkle with a few currants. Place on an ungreased baking sheet.

Bake for about 20 minutes, or until the pastry is puffed and lightly golden. Transfer the baking sheet to a wire rack and let cool for about 10 minutes, then drizzle the apples evenly with the syrup.

Carefully slip onto individual plates and serve warm.

SERVES 8

Classic Tarte Tatin

{pictured on the cover}

The origin of this famous tart lies with two French sisters, Caroline and Stephanie Tatin, proprietors of a charming inn in the small town of Lamotte-Beuvron, in the region of Orléanais, in the early years of the twentieth century. The area was known for its rustic apple tarts, but the *demoiselles* Tatin gained a reputation for baking the most extraordinary of the lot—an upside-down caramelized apple pastry that lured even Paris's fussiest palates. Our recipe comes from Paris chef Pascal Giraudeau (see page 75), who served a first-rate version of the sisters' legendary dessert at his cozy Chez Pascal in the fashionable fifth.

PASTRY

1 1/2 cups all-purpose flour

1 teaspoon sugar

1/4 teaspoon salt

1/2 cup chilled unsalted butter, cut into 1/2-inch pieces

3 to 4 tablespoons ice water

FILLING

7 tablespoons unsalted butter

2/3 cup sugar

1 tablespoon water

About 2 1/2 pounds assorted apples such as eastern Golden Delicious, Jonagold, Jonathan, York, or other good pie apples, peeled, halved or quartered (depending upon size), and cored

To make the pastry, stir together the flour, sugar, and salt in a bowl. Add the butter and cut in with a pastry blender until pea-sized particles form. Add the ice water, 1 tablespoon at a time, tossing and turning the mixture lightly with a fork to moisten the dough evenly. Use only as much water as is necessary for the dough to come together. Gently gather the dough into a ball and flatten into a thick disk. Wrap in plastic wrap and chill for about 2 hours.

To make the filling, melt the butter in an ovenproof 10-inch frying pan over medium-low heat. Add the sugar and water and stir until the mixture bubbles. Continue stirring until the mixture begins to brown, no longer than a few minutes, then remove from the heat and continue to stir for another minute until it turns a rich brown.

Arrange the apple pieces, rounded sides down, in the pan in a single layer, packing them tightly and creating an attractive pattern. The task is akin to laying bricks, and you may find that you need to cut some smaller pieces to fill in the gaps. Return the pan to the stove top over medium heat for 20 minutes to cook the apples partially. Remove from the heat and let cool for about 10 minutes.

Meanwhile, preheat the oven to 375°F.

To assemble and bake the tart, on a lightly floured work surface, roll out the dough about 1/8 inch thick and at least 1/2 inch larger in diameter than the frying pan. When the apples have cooled, drape the pastry round over the rolling pin and transfer it to the pan, letting it fall gently over the apples. Using your fingers—be careful not to burn them—tuck the edges of the pastry down inside the perimeter of the pan.

Bake for about 20 minutes, or until the crust is golden. Remove from the oven and let stand for about 5 minutes. Slip a knife between the edge of the crust and the pan to loosen it, if necessary. Invert a round serving plate (be sure it is at least 2 inches greater in diameter than the pan) on top of the pan and, holding the plate and pan together, flip them. Lift off the pan.

Serve the tart warm.

SERVES 6

VARIATIONS: For an extra, albeit nontraditional (in other words, Pascal would never do this) bit of apple flavor, sprinkle about 2 tablespoons Calvados over the apples after they have cooked for 20 minutes, ignite with a match, let the flames die out, and then continue as directed. For yet another flavor enhancement, which would doubtless turn the formal French apoplectic, pile a cup of sliced unpeeled apples at the center of the caramelizing apples. They'll be hidden between the crust and the pretty caramelized quarters or halves once the tart is turned out onto the serving plate.

Spice Tarte Tatin with Honey and Ginger

The first time I met Daniel Orr (see page 62) was at his apartment in the Chelsea district of Manhattan. A photo shoot was underway for his cookbook, *Daniel Orr Real Food*. "Who's this? His bodyguard or his gym trainer?" I thought, as a six-foot blond who looked like he belonged on the Norwegian wrestling team opened the door.

"Hi, I'm Daniel," he said, taking the armful of cider bottles I'd brought along for taste testing, one of which was French, one commercial American, and two from our farm in Kentucky. The athletic look wasn't accidental. During the two years that he trained at a series of French and Belgian restaurants, he realized his girth was growing quicker than his height, so he began running three miles between the lunch and dinner shifts. Back in New York at La Grenouille, he undertook two more conversions: he started every morning with a couple of hours at his neighborhood gym, and he gradually reinvented ultrarich classics like the *tarte Tatin* as lower—if not low—calorie dishes. Unlike the *demoiselles* Tatin, he uses no butter in the caramelizing, which should win at least some support from your cardiologist. It might outrage the old guard of French pâtisserie chefs, but when I made it for some Brooklyn friends, one of whom is a very strict English nurse, they all raved and demanded seconds.

(As for the cider tasting, our Kentucky version scored better on Daniel's palate than the commercially available American labels, but, not surprisingly, his favorite was the Pays d'Auge cider I'd carted back from Normandy.) —FB

1 cup honey

10 Granny Smith or Jonathan apples, peeled, quartered, and cored

2 tablespoons unsalted butter

1 tablespoon Sweet Season Spice Blend (see recipe introduction, page 62), or 1 teaspoon five-spice powder

2 teaspoons peeled, minced fresh ginger

1/2 teaspoon finely shredded lemon zest

Pinch of salt

1 sheet puff pastry, about 9 ounces, thawed if frozen, or rolled-out favorite pie pastry for a 9-inch pie

Sugar for sprinkling

1 teaspoon New Regime Spice Blend (see recipe introduction, page 62), or 1/2 teaspoon five-spice powder

3 tablespoons Armagnac or Calvados

CARAMEL SAUCE

1 1/2 tablespoons unsalted butter

1 cup sugar

6 tablespoons water

1/4 cup dark raisins, plumped in hot water and drained

1/4 cup golden raisins, plumped in hot water and drained

• • • • •

Crème fraîche as an accompaniment

To make the tart, place a high-quality 10-inch nonstick frying pan—a nonstick surface is important to keep the honey from sticking as it caramelizes—over high heat. When it is hot, pour in the honey and allow it to caramelize lightly. It is ready when it bubbles up and the froth begins to darken to a deep salmon, which will take about 5 minutes. Toss in the apples and cook, tossing often, for 8 to 10 minutes, or until they are evenly browned and are beginning to become tender.

Add the butter, Sweet Season blend, ginger, lemon zest, and salt and toss again to combine evenly with the apples. Remove from the heat and, being careful not to burn yourself on the hot honey, arrange the apples for final presentation. Return to high heat for about 5 minutes to caramelize for a final time. The honey and juices should be very shallow in the pan and create bubbles about 3/4 inch in diameter. Remove from the heat and let cool. (The dish can be made to this point up to several hours in advance and kept at room temperature.)

Preheat the oven to 375°F.

Once the apples have cooled, tear the pastry into 2- to 3-inch pieces and place them on top. The pieces can overlap, but avoid pressing them together, so that steam can escape as the tart cooks. Sprinkle the top with sugar and the Regime blend.

Bake for 20 to 25 minutes, or until nicely browned and cooked through. If the pastry begins to darken too much, cover loosely with aluminum foil.

While the tart is baking, make the caramel sauce: In a small, heavy saucepan, melt the butter over medium heat. Add the sugar and cook, stirring continuously, until the sugar melts and has begun to turn a golden brown. Gradually add the water and cook for 3 to 5 minutes, or until the mixture has a consistency slightly thicker than maple syrup. Remove from the heat and allow to cool. If the sauce thickens too much upon sitting, return it to medium heat and thin it with a little water, then let it cool.

Transfer the tart to a wire rack and let stand for 5 minutes. Then, using an insulated oven mitt to avoid burns, turn the tart out onto a large platter. If some of the apples and caramel have stuck to the pan, carefully scrape them out with a spoon or spatula and replace them in the tart. Sprinkle with the Armagnac. Stir the raisins into the caramel sauce and spoon over the tart.

Serve warm with a garnish of crème fraîche. Drizzle any remaining caramel sauce over the crème fraîche.

SERVES 8

Bourbon Apple Pie

To understand the particular perversity that makes Kentuckians who they are, I like to tell outsiders that you have to know that both Southern Baptists and bourbon began in Kentucky. Apple pies may symbolize purity, health, and clean living to many, but nothing complements the forbidden fruit better than adding a cup of good bourbon to the mix. The pie won't taste of the liquor after you've cooked it into the apples, but its contribution is diabolically rich. Serve this traditional dessert with a pitcher of clotted cream, and even the preacher will pretend not to notice. —FB

PASTRY

2 cups all-purpose flour

1/2 teaspoon salt

2/3 cup chilled solid vegetable shortening

3 tablespoons chilled unsalted butter

4 to 6 tablespoons ice water

FILLING

3 pounds mixed sweet and tart apples such as eastern Golden Delicious, Jonagold, or Fuji and Jonathan, Stayman Winesap, or Braeburn, unpeeled, halved, cored, and cut lengthwise into 1/2-inch-thick slices

1 cup sugar

1/2 teaspoon ground cinnamon

10 to 15 gratings nutmeg

1/2 teaspoon ground ginger

4 to 6 tablespoons unsalted butter

1 cup Maker's Mark or other fine Kentucky bourbon

2 teaspoons grated orange zest

• • • • •

1/2 teaspoon sugar

To make the pastry, stir together the flour and salt in a bowl. Add half each of the shortening and butter and cut in with a pastry blender until the mixture is the consistency of coarse meal. Then add the remaining butter and shortening and cut in until pea-sized particles form. Add the ice water, 1 tablespoon at a time, tossing and turning the mixture lightly with a fork to moisten the dough evenly. Use only as much water as is necessary for the dough to come together. Gently gather the dough into a ball, divide in half, and flatten each half into a thick disk. Wrap separately in plastic wrap and chill for about 1 hour.

To make the filling, place the apple slices in a large bowl. Sprinkle evenly with the sugar, cinnamon, nutmeg, and ginger, and stir and toss with 1 or 2 large spoons to coat the slices evenly.

In a large frying pan, melt the butter over medium heat. Add the apple slices and cook, turning as needed, for 5 to 10 minutes, or until beginning to turn golden. Add the bourbon and cook over medium heat for about 10 minutes, or until the apples are soft and the liquid is reduced to a light syrup. Stir in the orange zest. Let cool.

Preheat the oven to 400°F.

To assemble and bake the pie, place 1 dough disk on a lightly floured work surface and roll out into a 12-inch round about 1/8 inch thick. Drape the round around the rolling pin and transfer to a 10-inch pie pan, gently easing it into the bottom and sides. Trim the overhang so it extends about 1 inch beyond the rim of the pan, then fold the edges under. Roll out the remaining dough disk in the same manner for the top crust.

Spoon the filling evenly into the pie shell. Drape the second pastry round around the rolling pin and let it fall gently over the filling. Trim the overhang so it extends about 1/2 inch beyond the rim of the pie pan, fold the edge under, and flute attractively. Cut a few small vents in the top, then sprinkle the surface evenly with the sugar.

Bake for 10 minutes. Decrease the heat to 350°F and continue to bake for about 50 minutes longer, or until the pastry is golden. Transfer to a wire rack to cool. Serve warm.

SERVES 8

Rev. Henry Ward Beecher of Indiana, rhapsodizing on the glory of an apple pie:

"The sugar suggesting jelly, yet not jellied, the morsels of apple neither dissolved nor yet in original substance, but hanging as it were in a trance between the spirit and the flesh of applehood . . . then, O blessed man, favored by all the divinities! Eat, give thanks, and go forth, 'in apple-pie order!'"

Mary Hester's Fried Apple Pies

Along the ridges and valleys of Kentucky, Virginia, and southeastern Ohio, Sunday breakfast was usually a big event. Breakfast, not brunch. Usually there would be sausage—both links and patties—scrambled eggs, biscuits, buckets of butter, and, for special occasions in the winter, country ham and fried pies. A good ham would have been hanging for six or eight months, preferably a year. The fried apple pies were made from fruit dried the previous summer (traditionally Maiden Blush in Kentucky and Virginia), laid out on screens on a tin roof or, later, inside an old junker car with the windows rolled up, where, on an August afternoon, the temperature would top 130°F. The official story was that you didn't start using the dried apples until all the fresh ones had been eaten up or gone bad. But around Mary Hester's house, they sometimes cheated and started just a little early (say Halloween). The rich, sweet dried apple filling was too irresistible. —FB

FILLING

1/2 pound dried apples

2 1/2 to 3 cups water, or more as needed

1 teaspoon ground cinnamon

1/2 teaspoon ground nutmeg

Granulated sugar to taste

PASTRY

2 cups all-purpose flour

1 teaspoon salt

1/2 cup solid vegetable shortening

1/2 cup water

• • • • •

Safflower or other flavorless vegetable oil for deep-frying

Confectioners' sugar for dusting

To make the filling, combine the dried apples with the water in a heavy saucepan and place over low heat. Bring to a gentle simmer, cover, and cook until the apples are the consistency of very thick preserves. The timing will vary depending upon how dry the apples are (it may take as little as 20 minutes or as long as 1 hour). Add more liquid as needed to prevent scorching and achieve the correct consistency. Remove from the heat and stir in the cinnamon and nutmeg. Taste and add sugar as needed. The amount will depend upon how sweet the apples are naturally. (Kentuckians like a very sweet filling, and Mary would add up to 2 cups at this point. We added about 1/2 cup.) Let cool completely.

While the apples are cooking, make the pastry: In a bowl, sift together the flour and salt. Add the shortening and cut in with a pastry blender until the mixture is the consistency of coarse meal. Sprinkle the water over the surface and toss and turn the mixture lightly with a fork to moisten the dough evenly. Gather the dough into a ball and flatten it into a thick disk. (Although Mary never chilled the dough, you may find that wrap-

ping it and slipping it into the refrigerator for a short stint will make it easier to roll out. Dividing the ball in half will also ease the rolling.)

To assemble and fry the pies, on a floured work surface, roll out the dough no more than 1/8 inch thick. Cut into 6-inch squares or rounds. Place about 2 tablespoons of the apple mixture in the center of each piece, run a dampened finger around the edge, fold over, and seal the edges closed with the tines of a fork. Prick each filled pastry with the fork 2 or 3 times to let steam escape during cooking. (If you have a little filling left over, it will keep in a covered container in the refrigerator for a week or so. It doubles nicely as a garnish for roasted game, poultry, or pork.)

Pour oil into a deep saucepan to a depth of 2 inches and heat to 360°F on a deep-frying thermometer. One or two at a time, carefully slip the pies into the hot oil and fry, turning once, for 3 to 4 minutes on each side, or until golden. Using tongs or a slotted utensil, transfer to paper towels to drain.

Dust with confectioners' sugar and serve hot or warm.

MAKES ABOUT 12 INDIVIDUAL PIES

Palma's Apple and Walnut Pastry

Palma Csicsery (née Tahy) grew up in a big family with a summer house on the shore of Hungary's idyllic Lake Balaton, one of the world's great shallow lakes. Swimmers like Palma think of it as paradise, a place where friends wade out a half mile, chatting and gossiping as they go, before it's deep enough to swim. "We had a big apple orchard to one side of the house," she recalled some years ago, "with many varieties. I remember light green Calvilles and my favorite, golden Reinettes streaked with red. But in spite of all those trees, the weekly milk cart delivered even more apples and sacks of hazelnuts. We made lots of salads and strudels and a large sheet pastry called *almás pite* filled with apples and walnuts and flavored with a little of the local Tokay." In her later years, Palma continued to reside near a large lake, but she lived alone in an apartment on the seventh floor of a government building for seniors in Ashtabula, Ohio, and the sliver of water visible from her balcony was the gridlocked Lake Erie.

PASTRY

2 cups all-purpose flour

1/4 teaspoon salt

1 cup chilled unsalted butter, cut into 1/2-inch pieces

2 egg yolks, lightly beaten

3 tablespoons sour cream

FILLING

4 or 5 Stayman Winesap, Jonathan, Northern Spy, Jonagold, or other good pie apples, or a mixture, peeled, quartered, cored, and thinly sliced

Juice of 1 or 2 lemons

1 1/2 to 3 tablespoons sugar, or to taste

Splash of Tokay or Riesling (optional)

2 cups walnuts, ground

• • • • •

1 egg yolk, beaten, for glaze

To make the pastry, sift together the flour and salt into a large bowl. Add the butter and cut in with a pastry blender until pea-sized particles form. Make a well in the center and add the egg yolks and sour cream to it. Using a fork, gradually work the wet ingredients into the flour mixture until evenly moistened. Then, using your hands, gently knead the mixture in the bowl until it comes together in a smooth dough. Divide in half and flatten each half into a thick disk. Wrap separately in plastic wrap and chill for about 1 hour.

Preheat the oven to 375°F.

To make the filling, place the apple slices in a large bowl. Add the lemon juice and sugar to taste along with the wine, and toss well to coat evenly.

To assemble and bake the pastry, place 1 dough disk between 2 sheets of parchment paper and roll out into a large, thin rectangle no more than 1/8 inch thick. Trim to a rectangle about 10 by 14 inches. Repeat with the remaining dough disk.

Peel off the top sheet of parchment from the first pastry sheet. Evenly sprinkle half of the walnuts over the pastry sheet to within 1/2 inch of the edge. Arrange the apples on top of the walnuts in an even layer about 1/2 inch deep. Sprinkle the remaining walnuts evenly over the top. Peel off the top sheet of parchment from the second pastry sheet, invert the pastry sheet over the apples, and peel off the second parchment sheet. Press the edges of the two pastry sheets together to seal, then trim the edges evenly and seal with the tines of a fork. (If you have a fluted pastry wheel, this can be done in one step.) Brush the top with the egg yolk glaze and prick in several places with fork tines.

Carefully transfer the filled pastry to a rimless baking sheet. You may leave it on the parchment sheet for baking, which makes the transporting easier. Bake for 40 to 45 minutes, or until a rich golden brown.

Transfer to a wire rack and let cool completely on the baking sheet. Transfer to a large serving plate and cut into squares.

SERVES 8

"The best English apples by long training know how to behave in a pie; they melt but do not squelch; they inform but do not predominate. The early apples, grateful as we are for their re-appearance, are not true pie-makers. . . .We pardon these adolescents, who do the best they can, but we pass on to the later autumn apples to find pie manners at their best. And what should an apple do in a pie? Well I think it should preserve its individuality and form, not go to a pale, mealy squash, but become soft and golden. In flavour it must be sharp or what's the use of your Barbados sugar?"

—Edward Bunyard, *The Epicure's Companion*, 1937

Niçoise Swiss Chard and Apple Pie

....

In the early eighties, I was living in San Francisco's North Beach, a colorful swatch of Italy in North America. Just down the hill from my apartment, catercorner from the Romanesque Saints Peter and Paul Roman Catholic Church, stood the Liguria Bakery, a no-nonsense purveyor of authentic focaccia and a traditional stop for parishioners (and the rest of us) after Sunday morning mass. In those days, the bakers also regularly made a few lattice-topped pies filled with Swiss chard, pine nuts, cheese, and raisins and dusted with confectioners' sugar, an intriguing blend of the sweet and the savory. The pies were always displayed in the front window, and I could never resist them.

A few years later, on a visit to Nice, I discovered the French counterpart of that Ligurian specialty, but most Niçoise cooks added some apples too, making the unusual pie a shoo-in for this book. Research turned up the notion that the use of Edam or Gouda can be traced to the early Dutch brandy traders who did business in southern France, a surprising adoption for a nation that takes its own *fromage* so seriously. Provençal cooks are surprisingly easygoing on when to serve this pie, too, simply reducing the amount of sugar for a first course.

Although the Liguria continues to thrive, crowded with customers patiently waiting for the bakers to cut the long slabs of fresh-from-the-oven focaccia into large, manageable squares, the chard-and-raisin pies are now absent from the front window: "Not enough people came in to ask for them any more," the Genoese counterman explained, as he secured my parcel of focaccia. "So now we only bake them around the holidays, and then only on special order." —SS

PASTRY

2¼ cups all-purpose flour

1 tablespoon sugar

½ teaspoon salt

½ cup chilled unsalted butter, cut into ½-inch pieces

1 teaspoon freshly squeezed lemon juice

2 egg yolks

6 to 7 tablespoons ice water

FILLING

2 pounds Swiss chard, white stems removed

¼ cup raisins or currants

¼ cup dark rum or Calvados

2 eggs

½ cup granulated sugar

4 Fuji or other sweet apples, about 2 pounds total weight

⅓ pound Gouda or Edam cheese, finely diced

6 tablespoons pine nuts

1½ teaspoons grated lemon zest

Freshly grated nutmeg

• • • • •

Confectioners' sugar for dusting

To make the pastry, stir together the flour, sugar, and salt in a bowl. Add the butter and cut it in with a pastry blender until pea-sized particles form. Mix together the lemon juice, egg yolks, and 4 tablespoons of the ice water and add to the flour mixture, 1 tablespoon at a time, tossing and turning the mixture lightly with a fork to moisten the dough evenly. Add more ice water as necessary for the dough to come together. Gather the dough into a ball, divide it in half, and flatten each half into a thick disk. Wrap separately in plastic wrap and chill for about 2 hours.

To make the filling, place the Swiss chard in a large saucepan with only the rinsing water clinging to the leaves, cover, place over medium heat, and cook, turning the leaves once or twice, until wilted, about 5 minutes. Drain well, let cool slightly, squeeze dry, and chop finely. Set aside.

In a small saucepan, combine the raisins and rum, bring to a boil, remove from the heat, and set aside to cool.

Preheat the oven to 375°F.

In a bowl, whisk together the eggs and granulated sugar. Peel, halve, core, and finely dice 3 of the apples and add to the bowl along with the Swiss chard, raisins and any remaining rum, cheese, pine nuts, and lemon zest. Mix well, add several gratings of nutmeg, and mix again.

To assemble and bake the pie, place 1 dough disk on a lightly floured work surface and roll out into a round about 12 inches in diameter and $1/8$ inch thick. Drape the round around the rolling pin and transfer to a 10-inch pie plate, gently easing it into the bottom and sides. Trim the overhang so it extends about 1 inch beyond the rim of the plate, then fold the edges under. Roll out the remaining disk in the same manner for the top crust.

Spoon the filling evenly into the pie shell. Peel, halve, core, and thinly slice the remaining apple and arrange the slices evenly over the top. Dust with several gratings of nutmeg. Drape the second pastry round around the rolling pin and let it fall gently over the filling. Trim the overhang so it extends about $1/2$ inch beyond the rim of the plate, fold the edge under, and flute attractively. Cut a few small vents in the top.

Bake for about 40 minutes, or until the pastry is golden. Transfer to a wire rack to cool. Dust with confectioners' sugar and serve lukewarm or at room temperature.

SERVES 8

"Good apple pies are a considerable part of our domestic happiness."

—Jane Austen, 1815

Welsh Apple and Orange Pie

Oranges were among the favored treats of commoners in the Renaissance. So-called orange girls sold them at the gates to the Globe Theatre at Shakespeare's openings, a complement to the apples that were the ubiquitous fruit of the European peasantry. One of the most surprising and beguiling pies we came across while researching this Baedeker to apple cuisine comes from an old Welsh cookbook, *The Good Huswifes Handmaid for Cookerie*, published in 1588. Like most venerable recipes, this one provided only a sketchy guide to the pie's actual preparation, which among other things, included the following instructions:

> *Take your orenges and lay them in water a day and a night, then seeth them in faire water and honey and let seeth till they be soft; then let them soak in the sirrop a day and a night: then take forth and cut them small and then make your tart ... then lay on the lid and put it in the oven and when it is almost baked, take Rosewater and sugar and boyle them together till it be somewhat thick, then take out the Tart and take a feather and spread the rosewater and sugar on the lid and let it not burn.*

While this pie does take a little planning—you've got to start two days in advance of serving—it's easy to make and is infinitely adaptable for the adventurous cook. Try adding raisins, walnuts, or even cranberries, or experiment with bitter Seville oranges or tangy blood oranges. Like the Renaissance, its secret is that it marries elegance to simplicity.

5 thin-skinned oranges such as Valencia, Seville, Blood, or Temple

1 cup honey

PASTRY

2¹⁄₄ cups all-purpose flour

1 tablespoon sugar

¹⁄₂ teaspoon salt

¹⁄₂ cup chilled unsalted butter, cut into ¹⁄₂-inch pieces

2 egg yolks

6 to 7 tablespoons ice water

• • • • •

1 to 2 tablespoons cornstarch

5 medium to large mixed sweet and tart apples such as Gala, Pink Lady, Jonagold, Stayman Winesap, Jonathan, Newtown Pippin, and Granny Smith, unpeeled, halved, cored, and cut crosswise into ¹⁄₄-inch-thick slices

1 cup plus 2 tablespoons sugar

1 teaspoon ground cinnamon

³⁄₄ teaspoon ground ginger

1¹⁄₂ tablespoons unsalted butter, cut into small bits

¹⁄₄ cup rose water

In a large bowl, soak the unpeeled oranges in water to cover for 24 hours.

Transfer the oranges and their soaking water to a nonreactive saucepan and add the honey. Place over medium heat, bring to a simmer, and cook, uncovered, for about 40 minutes, or until the skins are soft when pricked with fork tines. Remove from the heat, return the oranges and cooking liquid to the bowl, and let cool. Weight down the oranges with a plate topped with a food can or other object to keep them submerged. Let stand for 24 hours. (They may be held in the syrup for up to 3 days before using.)

To make the pastry, stir together the flour, sugar, and salt in a bowl. Add the butter and cut in with a pastry blender until pea-sized particles form. Mix together the egg yolks and 4 tablespoons of the ice water and add to the flour mixture, 1 tablespoon at a time, tossing and turning the mixture lightly with a fork to moisten the dough evenly. Add more ice water as necessary for the dough to come together. Gently gather the dough into a ball, divide in half, and flatten each half into a thick disk. Wrap separately in plastic wrap and chill for about 2 hours.

To assemble and bake the pie, remove the softened, sweetened oranges from the liquid. Cut 2 of the oranges crosswise into thin slices, then cut the slices in half to form half-moons. Reserve on a plate. Chop the remaining 3 oranges into small pieces, capturing the juice, and place in a bowl. Stir the cornstarch into the chopped oranges to thicken the juice; the amount will depend upon how much juice the oranges release. Allow to stand for a few minutes.

Preheat the oven to 400°F.

Place 1 dough disk on a lightly floured work surface, and roll out into a round about 1/8 inch thick and at least 11 inches in diameter. Drape the round around the rolling pin and transfer to a 9-inch pie pan, gently easing it into the bottom and sides. Trim the overhang so it extends about 1 inch beyond the edge of the pie pan, then fold the edges under. Roll out the remaining disk about 1/8 inch thick and at least 12 inches in diameter. (The pie will be quite high, so you will need a large top crust.)

Prick the bottom crust in a few places with fork tines, then bake for about 10 minutes, or until the dough is set but has not yet colored. If the dough puffs up, press it down with the palm of your hand. (Slip on a clean oven mitt first if you aren't used to battling hot pastry with your bare hand.) Transfer to a wire rack to cool completely. Leave the oven set at 400°F.

Place the apple slices in a large bowl. In a small bowl, stir together 1 cup of the sugar, the cinnamon, and the ginger. Add to the apples and stir to distribute evenly.

Arrange a tight-fitting layer of apple slices in the pie shell. Top with a layer of the orange slices, again arranging them snugly. Add another layer of apple slices, and top with the chopped oranges. Add another layer of apples, another of orange slices, and then a final layer of apples. Dot the top with the butter. Drape the second pastry round around the rolling pin and let it fall gently over the filling. Trim the overhang so it extends about 1/2 inch beyond the rim of the pan, fold the edge under, and flute attractively. Cut a few small vents in the top.

(continued)

Bake for 10 minutes. Decrease the heat to 350°F and continue to bake for about 50 minutes, or until the crust is golden and the fruit juices have thickened to a thin syrup and are visible bubbling up through the slits.

While the pie is baking, in a small saucepan, stir together the rose water and the remaining 2 tablespoons sugar. Place over medium heat, bring to a simmer, and simmer for 4 to 5 minutes, or until a light syrup forms. Remove from the heat.

About 5 minutes before the pie is finished baking, brush the top crust with the rose water syrup. When the pie is done, transfer to a rack to cool. Serve warm.

SERVES 8

Faux Tarte au Citron

When our friend Annette was growing up in Paris under the Vichy regime, her family sent her into hiding in several countryside homes along the Loire Valley. It was hardly a happy time for her, but one of the strange and wonderful treats she came across was a *tarte au citron*—a lemon tart—but made with apples. Its provenance within French culinary tradition remains murky, but, she says, one possibility is that her protectors had learned to substitute the ever-available apple to help supplant the wartime scarcity of lemons. Whatever the true explanation, the fine blending of flavors in this tart is unique among apple desserts.

For the prettiest result, select McIntosh, Cortland, or other apples that do not turn brown when cut.

PASTRY

1 cup all-purpose flour

Pinch of salt

6 tablespoons unsalted butter, cut into ½-inch pieces

About 6 tablespoons ice water

FILLING

4 egg yolks

1¼ cups superfine sugar

Grated zest and juice of 1 large lemon

2 apples (see recipe introduction for suggested varieties), about 1 pound total

To make the pastry, stir together the flour and salt in a bowl. Add the butter and cut in with a pastry blender until pea-sized particles form. Add the ice water to the flour mixture, 1 tablespoon at a time, tossing and turning the mixture lightly with a fork to moisten the dough evenly until the dough comes together. Gently gather the dough into a ball, flatten into a thick disk, wrap in plastic wrap, and chill for about 2 hours.

Place the dough disk on a lightly floured work surface and roll out into a 10-inch round about ¹⁄₈ inch thick. Drape the round around the rolling pin and transfer it to a 9-inch tart pan with a removable bottom, gently easing it into the bottom and sides. Run the rolling pin over the top of the pan to trim off the excess pastry. Refrigerate until needed.

Preheat the oven to 350°F.

To make the filling, place the egg yolks in a bowl. Gradually add the sugar, beating constantly with a whisk or a handheld mixer at medium speed for about 3 minutes, or until very pale yellow and thickened enough to fall back into the bowl in a slowly dissolving ribbon when the beater is lifted. (Do not overbeat, or the yolks will turn granular.) Stir in the lemon zest.

Peel, quarter, and core the apples, then cut the quarters in half crosswise and place in a food processor. Process, gradually adding the lemon juice through the feed tube, until reduced to a pulp. Stir the apples into the egg mixture, mixing well. Pour the filling into the tart shell.

Bake for 35 to 40 minutes, or until the surface is uniformly golden and the filling is set. To test, plunge a thin-bladed knife into the center; it should come out clean. Transfer to a rack to cool. Slip off the sides of the tart pan and, using a wide spatula, carefully slide the tart onto a serving plate. Serve slightly warm or cold.

SERVES 6

Kentucky Apple Stack Cake

Apple stack cake crossed the Appalachian Mountains from Virginia with the first settlers in Kentucky, back when the state was just a western county of Virginia. It was the ideal year-round fruit-flavored cake in those days, well before either iceboxes or refrigerators, because it was made with dried apples. Mary Hester, who started at Browning Orchard as a teenager in 1949, learned how to make it from her mother and grandmother. "There were always two apple stack cakes at every Christmas celebration and family reunion, one made by my mother and one made by my grandmother Virginia," she once explained. "Mom would make her cake the day before, then she'd set it out on the porch in a cake box, so all the juices from the cooked, dried apples would soak into it. It never failed that when she brought the cake back in there was at least one slice missing. One of the boys—there were nine of us kids—had sneaked a piece out, because, well, with all those relatives around, sometimes seventy-five or a hundred, that might be the only way you'd get to taste it."

Dried apples were usually summer apples. Maiden Blush, a large, pale yellow apple with a pink cheek and an aromatic fragrance, was a favorite in Thomas Jefferson's orchard at Monticello because it dries particularly well in the midsummer sun. Mary's mother usually sun-dried several gallons for use in pies, fried turnovers, cakes, or for surreptitious nibbling. At the orchard we dried Maiden Blush, Wealthy, and Tydeman Red in the summer, but our favorite was an October apple, Stayman Winesap, well known for its sharp tang. Because the sun is low in the autumn, we dried the Winesaps in a dehydrator. —FB

CAKE LAYERS

3¹⁄₂ cups all-purpose flour, sifted

1 teaspoon baking soda

1 teaspoon ground cinnamon

1 teaspoon ground ginger

¹⁄₂ teaspoon ground nutmeg

¹⁄₂ teaspoon salt

¹⁄₂ cup unsalted butter, at room temperature

¹⁄₂ cup firmly packed brown sugar

1 cup sorghum or molasses

2 eggs, beaten

1 cup buttermilk

FILLING

1 pound dried apples, chopped

4 cups hard or fresh cider or water, or more as needed

Ground cinnamon and/or nutmeg

• • • • •

Confectioners' sugar for dusting (optional)

(continued)

Preheat the oven to 350°F. Butter and flour five 9-inch cake pans.

To make the cake layers, stir together the flour, baking soda, cinnamon, ginger, nutmeg, and salt in a medium bowl. In a large bowl, using a wooden spoon, mix together the butter and brown sugar until creamy. Add the sorghum and eggs and beat until well combined.

Add the flour mixture to the butter mixture in three batches, alternating with the buttermilk and beginning and ending with the flour mixture. The batter will be very stiff. Divide it evenly among the prepared pans, spreading it out with an icing spatula.

Kentucky lore is filled with apple seeds and romance: Press the seeds to your forehead, and the number that stick will be the number of days left before you see your sweetheart. Collect fresh, moist seeds, name them for your suitors, flip them in the air, and the one that strikes the ceiling is the one who loves you best. Name five seeds after boys you know, press the seeds to your face, and the first to fall will be the boy you marry.

Bake for 15 to 20 minutes, or until a wooden toothpick inserted into the center comes out clean. Transfer the pans to wire racks and let cool for 10 minutes, then turn the cakes out onto the racks and let cool completely. The cake layers will be thin, only about 1/2 inch high.

While the cake layers are baking, make the filling: Combine the dried apples with the cider or water in a heavy saucepan and place over low heat. Bring to a gentle simmer, cover, and cook until the apples are the consistency of relatively thick preserves. The timing will vary depending upon how dry the apples are. It may take as little as 20 minutes or as long as 1 hour. Add more liquid as needed to achieve the correct consistency. Flavor with a little cinnamon and/or nutmeg. Remove from the heat and let cool.

To assemble the cake, place a cooled cake layer on a serving plate. Spread one-fourth of the apple mixture evenly over the top. Top with a second layer and spread with one-third of the remaining apple mixture. Repeat with 2 more layers, dividing the remaining filling between them. Place the final cake layer on top. The apple mixture should be moist enough so that a little of the cooking juices dribble down the sides of the cake. Cover and let sit all afternoon or, better yet, a full day before serving.

Dust with confectioners' sugar (although Mary never would) just before serving.

SERVES 8

VARIATION: Substitute up to 1/2 cup rum for an equal amount of cider or water in the filling.

Maggie Gin's Apple-Nut Cake

Chinese sauce mogul and restaurateur Maggie Gin was an enviable whirlwind in the kitchen, able to pull ingredients off shelves and bake up a legion of book-worthy cakes—and just about everything else—without ever looking at a recipe. When I asked her if she had any good apple cake recipes, she immediately responded by e-mail, delivering a formula that seemed just fine. I whipped up the batter and baked it, only to have it turn out too dark and sinister, more appropriate for a Long March knapsack than an afternoon tea. I hit the send button, then immediately realized that the problem may have been my dark Bundt pan, which automatically dictates a lower oven temperature. But it was too late. Within an hour and a half, Maggie was on the doorstep, a warm apple cake in one hand and a revised recipe in the other. Now there was coffee and no buttermilk, orange zest and no brown sugar, more baking powder and less soda, and spoonfuls of other changes. As she sped back down the front stairs and drove out of sight, I heard her call out one last piece of advice: "Don't forget the scoop of vanilla ice cream with every slice." —SS

4 cups peeled, cored, and diced Rome Beauty, Jonathan, Newtown Pippin, or Granny Smith apples (1/2-inch dice)

1 cup coarsely chopped walnuts or pecans

1/2 cup unsalted butter, at room temperature

1/4 cup corn oil

1 1/2 cups sugar

3 eggs

1/2 cup cold, strong brewed coffee

3 cups unbleached all-purpose flour

1 teaspoon baking soda

2 teaspoons baking powder

1 teaspoon ground cinnamon

1 teaspoon freshly grated nutmeg

1/4 teaspoon ground ginger

1 teaspoon grated orange zest

Grease a 12-cup Bundt pan with butter. Preheat the oven to 350°F, or to 325°F if your pan is dark.

In a large bowl, toss together the apples and nuts. In a medium bowl, combine the butter, corn oil, and sugar and beat until smooth. Add the eggs and coffee and beat until creamy.

In another medium bowl, sift together the flour, baking soda, baking powder, cinnamon, nutmeg, ginger, and orange zest. Add the flour mixture to the butter mixture in three batches, mixing well. The mixture will be very thick. Pour the batter over the apple mixture and stir until evenly blended. Turn into the prepared pan.

Bake for 50 to 60 minutes, or until the cake springs back when pressed with your fingertip. Place on a wire rack and let cool in the pan for 10 minutes. Then turn out onto the rack to cool. Serve warm or at room temperature.

SERVES 8

Queensland Apple Cake and Custard Sauce

Tuny Walker was raised in the Australian outback, in Queensland, about 250 miles from Brisbane, where her family raises Herefords and cares for a couple of venerable apple trees. One fall day, Tuny's mother, faced with a surplus of Australia's own fine Granny Smiths, decided to revamp her tried-and-true single-layer cake into this scrumptious apple cake. It has become a family classic, although with seven kids one cake doesn't suffice. Tuny passed her mother's recipe along to us, explaining that the Walkers eat the moist, pretty cake for dessert with the custard sauce or for morning or afternoon tea without the sauce.

2 large Granny Smith or other tart apples

Juice of 1 large lemon

1 cup self-rising flour

³/₄ cup granulated sugar

5 to 6 tablespoons unsalted butter, at room temperature

¹/₂ cup milk

2 eggs, lightly beaten

³/₄ teaspoon vanilla extract

Ground cinnamon for dusting over cake

About 3 tablespoons superfine sugar for dusting over cake

CUSTARD SAUCE

1 cup milk

4 egg yolks

4 teaspoons granulated sugar

¹/₂ teaspoon vanilla extract

To make the cake, peel, halve, and core the apples, then cut lengthwise into thin slices. Place in a bowl with the lemon juice and toss to coat evenly. Set aside.

Preheat the oven to 350°F. Butter the bottom and sides of an 8-inch cake pan. Line the bottom with parchment paper and butter the paper.

In a bowl, combine the flour, granulated sugar, and 3 tablespoons of the butter, cut into 3 or 4 pieces. Using an electric mixer set on medium speed, beat until the butter breaks up into small pellets coated with the flour and sugar. Add the milk, eggs, and vanilla and beat until blended and smooth. Pour into the prepared cake pan and arrange the apple slices in concentric circles or other attractive pattern on top.

Bake for about 40 minutes, or until the cake is golden and springs back when pressed with your fingertip. Transfer the cake, still in the pan, to a rack.

Just as the cake is removed from the oven, melt the remaining 2 to 3 tablespoons butter. Dust the top of the hot cake with the cinnamon and superfine sugar and drizzle the hot butter evenly over the surface. Let the cake cool completely. Run a knife along the inside of the cake pan, then invert a serving platter over the cake.

Invert the pan and platter together, lift off the pan, peel off the parchment, and immediately turn the cake upright.

To make the custard sauce, pour the milk into a heavy saucepan and place over medium heat until small bubbles appear along the edges of the pan. Meanwhile, in a bowl, whisk together the egg yolks and granulated sugar until lemon colored and thick. Gradually whisk in the hot milk, then return the mixture to the saucepan over low heat. Cook, stirring constantly, for 8 to 10 minutes, or until the mixture thickly coats the spoon. To test, draw your finger along the back of the spoon; it should leave a trail. Remove from the heat and pour through a fine-mesh sieve into a clean bowl. Stir in the vanilla.

Serve the cake with the warm sauce.

SERVES 6

"There is no kind of Fruit better known in England than the Apple, or more generally cultivated. It is that Use, that I hold it almost impossible for the English to live without it, whether it be employed for that excellent Drink we call Cider, or for the many Dainties, which are made of it in the Kitchen. In short, were all other Fruits wanting us, Apples would make amends."

—Richard Bradley,
    British horticulturist, 1718

Apple Sorbet with Ginger

This big batch of refreshing pink sorbet (its lovely color the result of cooking the apples unpeeled) was gobbled right up by a legion of none-too-shy friends at one of our periodic apple-recipe tastings. Of course, you can easily cut the recipe in half, which leaves the hardworking cook the rest of the wine to sip when the crowd finally goes home. In either case, don't be cheap when it comes to buying the Gewürztraminer, or your fancy sorbet will taste like sherbet dished up at a freeway truck stop.

4 pounds assorted red-skinned apples such as Stayman Winesap, Jonathan, Braeburn, and Northern Spy

1¹/₂-inch piece fresh ginger

1 bottle (750 ml) good-quality Gewürztraminer

1 cup sugar

> At nineteenth-century "paring bees," a young woman would toss a piece of pared apple skin over her shoulder, hopeful that it would form the first letter of her future husband's name.

Cut the apples into sixths lengthwise, but do not peel or core. Place in a heavy saucepan. Lightly crush the ginger under the flat side of a knife to release its flavor, and add to the pan along with about 2 cups of the wine. Place over medium-high heat, bring to a steady simmer, and cook for about 15 minutes, or until the apples are soft. Add the sugar and stir until it dissolves, about 2 minutes. Remove from the heat and scoop out and discard the ginger.

Pass the cooked apples and their liquid through a food mill fitted with the fine disk, placed over a bowl. Stir in the remaining wine, cover, and refrigerate until chilled, about 2 hours.

Transfer the chilled mixture to an ice cream maker and freeze according to the manufacturer's directions. Spoon into a container, cover, and place in the freezer until firm, about 2 hours.

Spoon into clear glass bowls to serve.

MAKES ABOUT 2 QUARTS

Witches' Froth

....

The Hungarians usually serve this featherweight sweet, which they call *boszorkányhab*, after a big, rich meal of *gulyás* and dumplings or wild boar with sour cream. (The Kentucky bourbon, of course, is a Browning touch that no Hungarian would ever consider.) But if you've shown restraint on the main course, you might dress up this airy concoction by spooning it on top of individual meringues and then drizzling the servings with a sauce of puréed blueberries.

5 assorted small baking apples such as
Black Twig, Stayman Winesap, and Jonathan

1/2 teaspoon vanilla extract

2 egg whites

3/4 cup sugar

1 tablespoon Kentucky bourbon or applejack

"King's daughter, bid farewell to your maidenhood and weep not at its passing away for the tree that brings forth lusty apples is worth more than the one that but blooms."

—Pre-Renaissance French folk
quatrain, translated by David Sharp

Preheat the oven to 375°F.

Place the apples in a baking dish and add a couple spoonfuls of water to the dish. Bake for about 45 minutes, or until the apples are very soft and have begun to collapse. Remove from the oven and let cool.

Cut the apples into pieces and put them through a food mill placed over a bowl. Let cool completely. Stir in the vanilla.

In a bowl, using an electric mixer, beat the egg whites until frothy. Gradually add the sugar, beating until stiff, glossy peaks form. Fold the beaten egg whites into the cooled apple purée, then beat the mixture for a few minutes until frothy. Add the bourbon or applejack and continue to beat for a few minutes longer until very light and frothy.

Cover and chill well. Spoon into clear glass bowls to serve.

SERVES 4 TO 6

Portuguese Rice Pudding, California Style

This is a cross-cultural pudding. The method mimics that of my Portuguese grandmother, who would cook the rice in water, drain it, and then add it to the milk, rather than cook it only in milk or in a mixture of milk and water. But the rice is Italy's celebrated arborio, the cardamom is native to India, and the aromatic dried apples, in my case, are from trees planted on a Kentucky ridge. —SS

4 cups milk

1/2 cup dried apples, chopped

1/2 cup sugar

2 strips orange zest, each about
3 inches long

5 cups water

1/2 cup arborio rice

3 egg yolks

Pinch of salt

1/2 teaspoon vanilla extract

Ground cardamom for dusting over pudding

In a saucepan, combine the milk, apples, sugar, and orange zest over medium heat. Cook, stirring to dissolve the sugar, until small bubbles appear along the edges of the pan. Remove from the heat and set aside for 20 to 30 minutes.

Meanwhile, in another saucepan, bring the water to a boil. Add the rice, reduce the heat to low, and simmer gently for about 15 minutes, or until the rice kernels are plump and tender. Drain well.

Return the saucepan holding the milk and apples to medium heat and bring to a simmer. Add the drained rice and simmer, uncovered, stirring often, for about 20 minutes, or until thickened. Remove from the heat and remove and discard the orange zest.

In a bowl, beat together the egg yolks until light. Gradually whisk in about 1 cup of the hot rice mixture, then slowly whisk the mixture back into the saucepan. Add the salt and vanilla and cook over very low heat, stirring constantly, for about 5 minutes.

Remove from the heat and pour into a large serving bowl or individual bowls, spreading the rice evenly in the bowl(s). Let cool, cover, and chill. Dust with cardamom just before serving.

SERVES 6 TO 8

Apple Fritters, in the Manner of Cardano al Campo

A century ago, my mother's parents emigrated from the far north of Italy, traveling from the unremarkable village of Cardano al Campo, an austere Romanesque church its only notable architecture. They were leaving Lombardy, which has never made a name for itself in the apple world, although the higher reaches of neighboring Piedmont, Emilia-Romagna, and Veneto all boast respectable crops. Yet my grandmother was carrying the secret of wonderfully light apple fritters, narrow fruit slices coated in a thin batter scented with lemon, when she arrived at Ellis Island, and she passed it along to her daughter, who, in turn, gave our orchard apples a lovely Italian accent. —SS

1 cup all-purpose flour

Pinch of salt

1 medium egg

$1/2$ cup plus 2 tablespoons milk

$1/2$ cup plus 2 tablespoons water

Grated zest of 1 lemon

Safflower oil or other flavorless vegetable oil for deep-frying

3 large Granny Smith, Newtown Pippin, or other tart apples, peeled, cored, and thinly sliced lengthwise

Superfine sugar for coating fritters

In a bowl, sift together the flour and salt. Make a well in the center and break the egg into it. Stir the egg into the flour until well mixed. In a measuring pitcher, stir together the milk and water. Gradually add the milk-water mixture to the flour mixture, beating constantly until smooth. Stir in the lemon zest. Cover and refrigerate for 1 hour.

Pour oil into a deep saucepan to a depth of 2 inches and heat to 360°F on a deep-frying thermometer. Stir the apples into the batter. Working in small batches, lift out the apple slices with tongs or chopsticks and add to the hot oil. Fry, turning once, for about 2 minutes total, or until pale golden. Using the tongs or chopsticks, transfer to a wire rack placed over a plate to drain briefly.

Spread the sugar on a plate and turn the hot apple fritters in the sugar to coat evenly. Serve piping hot.

SERVES 6

Apples Stuffed with Goat Cheese
and Crystallized Ginger

There was a time when goat cheese in America was as rare as an honest politician, but nowadays even many supermarkets stock a label or two. In the San Francisco Bay Area, small farms and creameries in Sonoma and Marin counties make goat cheeses so good that the local French chefs use them without apology. We are campaigning to have those same chefs wed that bumper crop of chèvre to the region's best baking apples. It's a decidedly delicious romance, as this recipe, inspired by one created by talented food and garden writer Georgeanne Brennan, illustrates.

6 Rome Beauty, Stayman Winesap, or other quick-baking apples

¾ pound soft fresh goat cheese, at room temperature

About 5 tablespoons firmly packed golden brown sugar

¼ cup chopped crystallized ginger

2 tablespoons toasted chopped pistachios

Preheat the oven to 375°F. Select a baking dish just large enough to accommodate the apples standing upright.

With a melon baller or grapefruit spoon, scoop out the core from each apple, being careful not to pierce the blossom end, and discard. Then continue to scoop out the apple flesh to form a hollow cavity about 1½ inches in diameter with sturdy sides. Reserve the removed pulp for another use or discard.

In a bowl, stir together the goat cheese and brown sugar until smooth. Taste and adjust the amount of sugar to taste. Stir in the crystallized ginger. Spoon the cheese mixture into the apples, filling each one generously. Place in the prepared baking dish and sprinkle the pistachios evenly over the top. Pour water to a depth of about ⅓ inch in the bottom of the dish.

Bake for about 30 minutes, or until the apples are fully tender when pierced with a fork and the tops are browned. Serve immediately.

SERVES 6

Baked Apples with Port

Although port is clearly part of Silva's patrimony—Browning's Anglo forebears traveled to Silva's Porto as early as the twelfth century to load ships with the fortified *vinho*—Browning came up with this modest but comely baked apple dessert that celebrates Iberia's sweet, warming wine.

6 Jonathan, Stayman Winesap, Rome Beauty, Jonagold, or other good baking apples

3 tablespoons unsalted butter

1/3 cup sugar plus 2 tablespoons

About 1/4 teaspoon ground ginger

About 2/3 cup port

1/2 cup water

Heavy cream as an accompaniment

Newtown Pippins, first grown on Long Island in the mid-1700s and shipped to Benjamin Franklin in London, later became America's first export fruit to England. The variety was particularly favored by Queen Victoria.

Preheat the oven to 350°F. Select a baking dish just large enough to accommodate the apples standing upright.

With an apple corer or paring knife, remove the core from each apple, being careful not to pierce the blossom end, and discard. Place 1/2 tablespoon butter, 1 teaspoon sugar, and a pinch of ginger in each apple, then pour in enough port to fill the cavities.

Stand the apples in the reserved dish. Add the remaining 1/3 cup sugar to the dish, distributing it evenly around the apples. Then pour in the remaining port (it should be about 1/3 cup) and the water.

Bake for about 40 minutes, or until the apples are fully tender when pierced with a fork. Remove from the oven and let cool slightly.

Transfer the apples to individual plates and spoon the port sauce from the baking dish over them. Serve with a pitcher of cream for those who are not afraid of extra calories.

SERVES 6

Russian Summer Tea

Russians, says reporter Alex Van Oss, are the world's most resourceful entertainers. Give them a piece of fruit and a hunk of bread and they'll make a party. While on assignment for National Public Radio one hot August day several years ago, Van Oss was sweltering through an afternoon of bureaucratic appointments in Moscow. Finally, the official he'd been waiting to see ushered him into a private office.

"Let me offer you a cup of *lyetnii chai*, summer tea," the Russian proposed. "Oh God, hot tea in this heat!" Van Oss thought to himself. But, ever polite, he accepted the offer, and the bureaucrat's secretary disappeared. Moments later she returned bearing two steaming glass mugs of ordinary Russian black tea. On top of each floated a layer of finely diced—unpeeled—apple.

"It was utterly delightful, unbelievably cooling, and it filled my head with the most remarkable aromas," Alex reported. Now it has become a fixed part of his summer survival armament for muggy afternoons at home in Washington, D.C.

¼ **Gala, Williams' Red, Honeycrisp, Wealthy, Gravenstein, or other summer apple**

1 **pot freshly brewed black tea**

Core the apple quarter, but do not peel. Cut into fine dice. Put about 1 teaspoon of the apple into each mug and pour in the tea. Wait for about a minute, then serve. Sip and relax.

SERVES 4 TO 6

"No other fruit unites the fine qualities of all fruits as does the apple. For one thing, its skin is so clean when you touch it that instead of staining the hands it perfumes them. Its taste is sweet and it is extremely delightful both to smell and to look at. Thus by charming all our senses at once, it deserves the praise that it receives."

—Plutarch, *Table Talk V*

Lexington Paluda

When Marc Sharifi was a boy growing up in Lexington, Kentucky, having recently emigrated from Iraq, his mother helped salve the stresses of relocation with this refreshing memory of their homeland. In Iran and Iraq, it is traditionally made as a dessert, without the water. But when the Sharifis were faced with Kentucky's heat and humidity, they converted *paluda* into a tall, cool beverage.

1 McIntosh, Gala, Honeycrisp, or other late-summer apple, peeled, quartered, and cored

Juice of 1/2 lemon

1/4 cup superfine sugar

1 tablespoon rose water

3 cardamom seeds

4 cups boiling water

Place the apple quarters in a bowl and toss with the lemon juice to prevent browning. (Marc, however, recommends letting them oxidize, as it makes a richer colored drink.) Finely grate the apple quarters and place in a heatproof pitcher. Add the sugar, rose water, and cardamom seeds, and pour in the boiling water. Stir until the sugar is fully dissolved. Let stand until cool, then cover and refrigerate until well chilled, or serve immediately over ice.

SERVES 4

HONEYCRISP

Traditional Kyrgyzstani women who failed to conceive would roll on the grass beneath an apple tree, hoping to make themselves fertile.

Moroccan Apple Sharbat

Because of their faith, most Moroccans do not drink alcoholic beverages, and at mealtimes they seem not to drink anything at all. "We can't drink too much liquid with dinner," explained a Moroccan gentleman, "or the couscous in our stomachs will swell." Cold lemonade or orangeade is drunk before and after meals, however, and a *sharbat*, a nut or fruit milk drink, is favored on hot afternoons when a cooling pick-me-up is in order. Almond milk, a rather sweet mixture of crushed almonds, sugar, water, milk, and orange flower water, is the most celebrated of the *sharbat* repertoire, but it is also quite costly because so many nuts are used. This apple *sharbat* is a cheaper, yet still quite refreshing, option for the Moroccan working stiff or schoolboy.

2 or 3 McIntosh, Gala, Cortland, Honeycrisp, or other sweet summer apples, peeled, cored, and diced

2¹/₂ tablespoons sugar

1¹/₂ teaspoons orange flower water

2¹/₂ cups chilled milk

Crushed ice

In a blender, combine the apples, sugar, orange flower water, and milk. Process until smooth. Pour over crushed ice in glasses.

SERVES 4

Thomas Knight and his daughter, Frances, produced the first man-made apple crosses in the 1790s, using the Golden Pippin as the primary parent.

INDEX